A HATFUL OF MUSIC

THE DANCE BAND DAYS IN
LUTON, DUNSTABLE & DISTRICT

STUART GOODYEAR

The Book Castle

First published November 2003 by
The Book Castle
12 Church Street
Dunstable
Beds LU5 4RU

ISBN 1 903747 42 2

Designed and typeset by Caroline and Roger Hillier
The Old Chapel Graphic Design

Back cover photograph of author © Roger Hillier

Printed by Antony Rowe Ltd., Chippenham, Wiltshire

Contents

I wish to sincerely thank the following people and organisations, without whose help, the compilation of this book would not have been possible.

Ray Aldous; Lillian Armstrong; Rita Arnold; Pat Ayres; Bob Bates; Jean Billington; Barbara Bird; Connie Blain; John 'Jerry' Blain; Gerry Bohan; Diane Brown; Elizabeth Brown; Keith Burgoine; Stephen Chamberlain; John Collier; The Co-operative Bank; Dankworth Management; Fenwicks; First Garden City (Letchworth) Heritage Museum; Mark Fischer; Ron Franks; Diana Godfrey; Kenny Gorrell; Peter Green; Bob Groom; Jimmy Harrison; Edna Hendley; Rachael Hibbert; Edwina Hillier; Stuart Horn; Derek Hunt; Keith Indge; David Johns; Doug Jones; Roy Joyner; Peter Lock; John Lovesey; Luton Museum Service; The Luton News; Jimmy Marsh; Kath McDavitt; Chris Morris; John Murray; Les Old; Rob and Joyce Perrins; Connie Peters; Brian Sapwell; Ken & Janet Scott; John Scott; Bill Seaford; Paul Sims; South Bedfordshire District Council; Jimmy Stead; Ken Tibbs; Tommy Thompson; The Vauxhall Mirror; Victoria & Albert Museum Picture Library; Les Walters; Freddie Wells; Keith Willison and Margaret, my patient wife, who dutifully typed and retyped so many pages, and of course, Peter Thompson.

Mum & Dad

Mum came to Hertfordshire in the late 1920s from the coal-mining village of Burradon in Northumberland with her sister and cousins to escape the hardship of employment in the area – especially for young females.

Elizabeth 'Betty' Bland found work in service (i.e. cooking, washing-up and cleaning etc.) at Hartsbourne Manor Golf Club, Bushey Heath, Watford and joined her elder sister Nance (Annie), who was already here. At weekends she worked at the many functions requiring waitresses and cooks etc., and it was in this environment that she was to meet a visiting bandleader (and hat manufacturer) from Luton – Stuart John Goodyear, of Windmill Road. This would have been about

Mum & Dad.

LORD AMPTHILL LODGE, No. 1759, R.A.O.B.

Concert & Social Evening
on behalf of the Children's Party

at the R.A.O.B. CLUB, Bute St.,
Thursday, Aug. 12
Commencing at 7-45 p.m.

SONNY GOODYEAR'S MUSICAL FOUR
BARBARA LOVELL
The well-known Local Soprano
STUART GOODYEAR
Violin

Numerous Surprise Items
Tickets 6d.
OBTAINABLE AT THE BAR

Poster for a 1937 concert. Sonny (cousin), Barbara and Dad on the same programme. (R.A.O.B = Royal Antediluvian Order of Buffaloes).

1936/7, and they may well have met at Harpenden Common Golf Club, where she was known to work regularly at weekends.

I also remember Dad and Mum in later years speaking with affection about, and often visiting, Bob Peters, who was the Secretary and Club Professional at Harpenden Common Golf Club. They married in 1938, bought their home at 112 Walcot Avenue, Luton, for £495 (they paid the extra £5 for garage space!), and I was born in 1939.

Dad was a very talented musician, and was able to read music or busk, and play violin, accordion and double bass, with most of his accomplishments being through self-tuition. I later had to rely on my cousin Barbara* to fill me in on Dad's youth, as like all young men I was always too pre-occupied with my own importance to absorb his achievements and many talents, of which he spoke of very rarely, until it was too late.

As a lad, he played in the Luton Youth Band on violin, and was given tuition by the violinist leader Alf Huckle. They rehearsed upstairs at the 'Royal' in Mill Street, and performed regularly at the Central Mission.

To put into perspective his ability, he played Monti's 'Czardas' at a talent competition at the Palace Theatre, Mill Street, when he was about 19, and was accompanied by Barbara on piano, who remembers her mum buying her an emerald green skirt and blouse specially. Barbara, who was 4 years younger than Dad, said "We deserved better than runners up!!"

He ran the successful New Astorians dance band through the 1930s until his marriage, when, doubtless because of my arrival and mum's solitude in her new home at Luton, Dad unselfishly decided to finish with the band, to spend weekends with us. Of course unbeknown to them at the time, the 2nd World War was about to start anyway.

*Barbara Bird (née Lovell) was Dad's sister Victoria's eldest daughter, who, with husband Ron, also bought a house in Walcot Avenue (No.119) when they got married, and lived there all their lives, as did Dad until his death in 1992, at the age of 80.

Members of the "New Astorian" Dance band (mid 1930s),
l. to r.: Ron Whittaker (Piano Accordion); Sonny Goodyear (Sax, Trumpet); Stuart Goodyear (Snr) (Violin).

Although he had finished his band, he still played his beloved instruments at home, and I remember him taking Mum and me out to village pubs at weekends where he played the accordion to very appreciative locals. 'The Engineer', on the corner of St. John's Road and Cravells Road on Harpenden Common, was visited more often than most – Harpenden again!

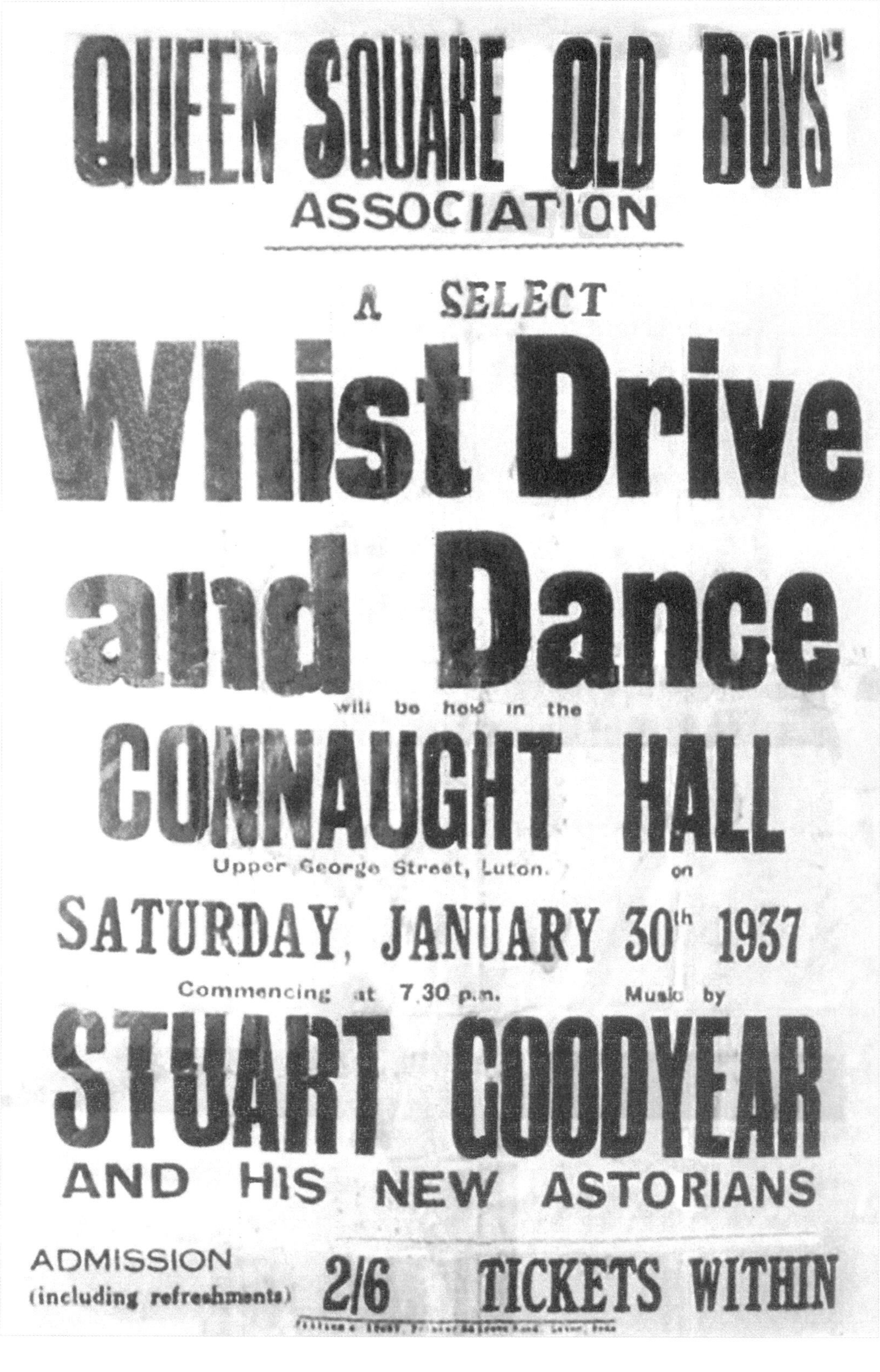

QUEEN SQUARE OLD BOYS'
ASSOCIATION
A SELECT
Whist Drive
and Dance
will be held in the
CONNAUGHT HALL
Upper George Street, Luton. on
SATURDAY, JANUARY 30th 1937
Commencing at 7.30 p.m. Music by
STUART GOODYEAR
AND HIS NEW ASTORIANS
ADMISSION
(including refreshments) 2/6 TICKETS WITHIN

Left Typical of the times, the "New Astorians" playing for a select whist drive and dance. The Connaught Hall was at 15/17 Upper George Street, above Arthur Day's Music Shop.

Right and Below A 1936 pre picked programme for a Saturday evening social at the Bobbers Stand Club, Luton Town F.C., which is a good example of 1930s dance music, as supplied by "The New Astorian Dance Band".

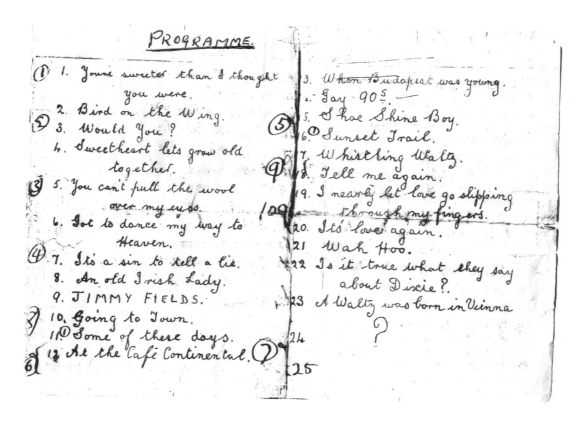

THE
NEW ASTORIAN
DANCE BAND
AT THE
BOBBERS STAND CLUB
ON
SAT. OCT 17ᵗʰ 1936
LEADER.
STUART GOODYEAR.

STUART GOODYEAR   VIOLIN & BASS.
RON WHITTAKER   PIANO ACCORDIAN
SON GOODYEAR   SAX. TRUMPET &
                         VOCALIST
EDDIE SAUNDERS   PIANIST
ALEC SIMMS   DRUMS
JIMMY FIELDS   ENTERTAINER

PROGRAMME.

1. You're sweeter than I thought you were.
2. Bird on the Wing.
3. Would You?
4. Sweetheart lets grow old together.
5. You can't pull the wool over my eyes.
6. Got to dance my way to Heaven.
7. Its a sin to tell a lie.
8. An old Irish Lady.
9. JIMMY FIELDS.
10. Going to Town.
11. Some of these days.
12. At the Café Continental.

3. When Budapest was young.
4. Gay 90ˢ.
5. Shoe Shine Boy.
6. Sunset Trail.
7. Whistling Waltz.
8. Tell me again.
19. I nearly let love go slipping through my fingers.
20. Its love again.
21. Wah Hoo.
22. Is it true what they say about Dixie?
23. A Waltz was born in Vienna?
24.
25.

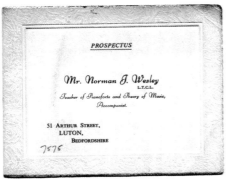
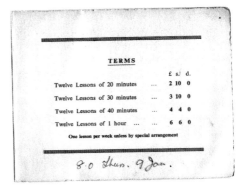

The 1950s Prospectus of Pianoforte teacher Norman Wesley.

When the war finished (1945) I guess Dad turned his thoughts to me, and decided I should have piano lessons. I remember him taking me over the road to see cousin Barbara, and talking her into teaching me — as her first pupil. Barbara went on to teach pianoforte for a further 50+ years, until well into her 80s. I went to Barbara for about five years, then transferred to May Gough's at 77 Reginald Street for advanced tuition until I was about 15. I then had a couple of years with Norman Wesley in Arthur Street, who, as a well established concert and dance band pianist on the local scene, did his best to smooth me out.

Mum went back home to 'Newcastle' at every opportunity — usually school holidays, and when Dad came too, he always made a point of visiting Fenwicks to see the resident band in the restaurant, which was of course the first live band I ever saw. I still go to Fenwicks, for some buttered scones and a pot of tea, as we did then, but unfortunately the band has long since gone.

Fenwick's Terrace Tea Room Orchestra

Above Shown here supported by the Vauxhall Orchestra, vocalist Barbara Bird starred in this early 1940s Sunday Concert in the main Vauxhall canteen, Kimpton Road, Luton. In the background is the Orchestra's musical Director and Conductor, Fred Green.

Left The first band I saw playing live music was the Fenwick's Tea Room Orchestra in Newcastle-Upon-Tyne, which I remember as the Willie Walker Band. This is a much earlier picture of Billy Ternent and the Terrace Tearoom Orchestra (c1925) playing 'Alabamy Bound'!

By 17 I had achieved the limits of my potential, but never anticipated the exciting and rewarding future that lay ahead. I found learning music difficult, and was never the 'natural' that Dad was, <u>but</u> through Mum's (strict) insistence and Dad's continual persuasion, I eventually (and very gratefully) became proficient on the keyboard. I mention Mum's strictness because she was the one who insisted I did my ½ hr. a day music practice, <u>and</u> she wasn't adverse to using the dog lead on my legs if I tried to dodge it. At the time I cursed, but she always said to me – "I never had the chance, you must take yours, Stuart" – Mum and Dad even bought the most beautiful piano for me, from Arthur Day's music shop in Upper George Street. It was a green and cream birds eye maple Hickie and Hickie 'Kemble' piano which was on centre display in their shop window. I never appreciated the sacrifices they must have made for me.

My eldest daughter Ruth playing 'The Kemble'.
(The sheet music is "Look for a Star"!)

Without their determination on my behalf, I know I would have ducked out of music at the first opportunity. To them, I dedicate this compendium of recollections.

January 2003

The Rainbow Melody Makers

My personal reminiscences of Luton and the dance scene range from the 1950s through to the early 80s, the period which covered my active participation. I will endeavour to portray things in general, but must be forgiven if I lapse into more personal accounts. To start with, I think it would be beneficial to explain exactly how things were, and how I started in the scene of semi-professional music, with some fellow engineering apprentices.

Big bands like Ted Heath, Tommy Dorsey, Ray Anthony, Edmundo Ros, and Glenn Miller were everybody's favourites, and they also supported the singing stars of the day, such as Dickie Valentine, Johnnie Ray, Frankie Lane, Frank Sinatra, Doris Day, Ella Fitzgerald and Anne Shelton etc.

During my apprenticeship at D. Napier & Son, Luton Airport, I played piano at a few social functions and stag evenings, and was approached by a fellow apprentice Ken Tibbs, who had taken up acoustic guitar, with the suggestion that we could form a small band. I was happy to join Ken, and found his enthusiasm quite intoxicating, especially his daily trips into the workshops at Napiers to see me and talk 'music'. Ken had almost finished his apprenticeship, and was working in the materials stress office.

After a few rehearsals it wasn't too long before Ken moved from guitar to tenor sax, which I believe was his father's. His progress was excellent, and to become the proficient sax player that he was, in such a short time, was most commendable. He still plays tenor to this day and, although he now lives in Biggleswade, still rehearses weekly with the (Luton) High Town Band.

Ken started arranging his sax parts from my piano copies, so all we needed now was somewhere to play – and a drummer. Through Dad, we started a Saturday/Sunday residency at the 'Specials' (Special Constables) Club in Williamson Street, Luton on the 26th February 1957. The members went round with the hat each evening to pay us!

The first drummer to play with Ken and me was Ray Lelliott who, with his parents, ran a provisions shop in Dallow Road. We were all 'green', but Ray had bigger and more immediate aspirations, and soon left to form his own 3–4-piece band – which he still runs today!

Ken Millard was the drummer with the Ronnie Pleydell Band at the Cresta Ballroom, and David's first drum tutor (c.1956). Born in Gillingham, Ken previously played with Harry Parry and Harry Leader at Butlins Resorts and, after the Cresta, joined Gene Mayo at Nottingham Palais and Harry Roy at the Tottenham Royal.

David Johns, who was an apprentice at our sister company English Electric, also at the Airport, was to join us in April 1957, and without doubt his keenness gave us an impetus to progress in a positive manner. He was also receiving the very finest drum tuition from the professional drummer at the plush Cresta Ballroom. The club called us The Rainbow* Melody Makers – again I think Dad had a hand in this.

The piano had seen better days, and what we sounded like, playing the popular dance numbers of the day such as 'Unforgettable', 'A White Sports Coat', 'Fascination', 'When I Fall In Love' and 'Beyond The Blue Horizon' etc., can only be imagined.

> DANCES
> —
> DINNERS
> —
> SOCIALS
> —
> PARTIES
>
> THE
> **RAINBOW**
> **MELODY MAKERS**
> **DANCE BAND**
>
> WRITE
> SECRETARY :
>
> S. J. GOODYEAR,
> 112, WALCOT AVENUE,
> LUTON, BEDS.

Our first business card.

*Rainbow Hall Farm, Flamstead was Dad's Great Grandfather's, Grandfather's and Father's home. When his father came to work at Luton as Powdrills Foreman, he was nicknamed 'Rainbow'. Our house in Walcot Avenue was called Rainbow House!

Serious Stuff! Playing at the Napier/English Electric Clubhouse, Crawley Green Road, Luton c.1959.

THE
"RAINBOW"
MELODY MAKERS
will be playing at
this Establishment on
SATURDAY EVENING
Please Come Along,
It is for Your Entertainment

You can't beat self publicity!

Right Playing at the 'Cock', Offley for Brenda Tibbs' (Ken's sister) pre-wedding party on 21st July 1960. Ken, on clarinet, is surrounded by family members and friends.

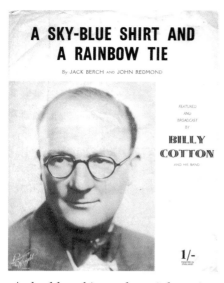

A SKY-BLUE SHIRT AND A RAINBOW TIE

By JACK BERCH AND JOHN REDMOND

FEATURED
AND
BROADCAST
BY

**BILLY
COTTON**

AND HIS BAND

1/-

A sky-blue shirt and a rainbow tie.

Dad went everywhere with us, and one song that he enjoyed us playing was "And you're all dolled up in a sky blue shirt, and a <u>rainbow</u> tie"!! (I wonder why?). Although the song was popular, it was a bit 'corny', but not for Dad.

Our trio had limitations, and an evening's engagement was hard work, so we had to expand, and anyway, we had caught the bug by now, and a larger outfit was a natural progression. We hadn't a book full of engagements, or the reputation to attract new personnel, and many a young musician came and went and rehearsed with us "week in/week out for nowt". To all of those musicians I shall be eternally grateful, as their participation gave us some experience of augmenting to get a bigger sound.

The 'Specials' allowed us to rehearse in their snooker room, which was OK, but on the 3rd floor. The stairs were steep and not very wide, and although the room was not easily accessible, the club's generosity was greatly appreciated. We were of course taking 10/12 drinkers into the club on a quiet night! It was a busy club, and, as a keen Luton Town F.C. supporter, I was pleased to see the Town's top goal scorer Gordon Turner using it. (How the club ever got a snooker table into that room, still remains a mystery).

Soon to join us was Brian Wiles on trumpet (and occasional vocal) who was the most amiable, willing and jovial of people, which was an asset in those early days, when some of our performances left a lot to be desired. Brian was the manager of credit drapers Dupont Bros in Rothesay Road, Luton, which often demanded unsociable hours of working, so Brian departed when he could not guarantee his presence at our weekly rehearsals and occasional bookings.

Another cousin Sonny Goodyear* grew up with Dad and was a great virtuoso on saxophone and trumpet, as well as being a superb vocalist. 'Son' had become a household name locally with his versatility both as an instrumentalist and compere/vocalist at the Alma cinema's Sunday evening concerts, and as Uncle Sonny at the Union Cinema's Saturday morning children's club. (The Union in Gordon St., was renamed The Ritz). The band that Son played with mostly during the 1940s and 50s was The New Collegians Dance Band, which also featured Billy Gilbert on trumpet and piano. Son's wife Lillian told me that the two numbers that he always sang, as being his favourites, were:
'When Day Is Done' and 'Just A Wearyin' For You'.

*Sonny was the eldest son of Dad's eldest brother Frederick. He was also christened Frederick Arthur after his Dad, but was called Sonny or Son all his life. He died in 1972.

The Collegians at the George Hotel. With George Smith (standing on the left) as manager, they were kept busy through the 1940s. Leader Derrick Smith (standing on the right) was George's son and Sonny Goodyear is on the saxophone. Others unfortunately unknown.

This line-up confirms the popularity of the Accordion Bands during the late 1930s into the 1940s. Personnel l. to r.: Ivor Zibrid; George Cooper; Jackie Wood (Drums); Billy Gilbert; Sonny Goodyear. And the K.T. on the bandstands? The Kingsway Tavern of course! The Kingsway was a very popular venue at that time. Through to the early 1960s, Sunday nights at The Tavern was " The Place to go" for the in-crowd. Budding singers were encouraged to take the mic., and there were none better than Nick Morrissey who was always on hand to sing the latest Johnny Mathis numbers.

Although Son was Dad's nephew, there was little age difference between them, and they were very close friends, especially in their formative years.

We (The Rainbow Melody Makers) were obviously delighted when Son agreed to play with us at the Specials Club on Saturday 11th May 1957. Ken on tenor sax, and Brian Wiles on trumpet were also on duty, and it was to be the only time we were honoured with Son's presence, but it gave us our first insight into having an experienced 'pro' in the line-up.

Eventually though one or two of the committee members at the club didn't really want us playing there and 'gave us the sack'. Dad was very upset, and on the last night told David on drums to "play as loud as you can".

LUTON UNITED LIBERAL & CONSERVATIVE ASSOCIATION

STOPSLEY WARD   ROUND GREEN SECTION

GRAND DANCE

SMALL HALL
LUTON TOWN HALL
SATURDAY, 18th JANUARY, 1958
8 p.m.   ::   Midnight
RAINBOW MELODY MAKERS

Licensed Bar   Admission 4/-

Hitting the big time! One of our first commercial bookings.

At the tail end of 1957 we picked up one or two work associated and family bookings which kept our enthusiasm on a roll, but the first engagement "to meet the outside world" was to be in the 'Small Assembly Hall' at the Luton Town Hall on Saturday 18th January 1958 for the local Liberal/Conservative Association. The booking was given to us by Mrs. Bradbury (next door neighbour) and Mrs. Taylor from Taunton Avenue, who were the two 'mainstays' and social organisers of the ward committee.

The preparation for the dance was very thorough, and I made sure that I had every possible request in my library, having "never been there before" i.e. Gay Gordons; Palais Glide and Paul Jones etc. etc. Sensibly it was felt that an 'old hand' should be booked to play in the band, and Dad called on his old friend and popular band leader Geoff Stokes to sit in with us on alto sax. (It was a miracle he was available and willing to play!). We sold over 50 tickets for the dance, calling on all of our friends to swell the crowd for moral support. The dance was a financial success, but I don't know who was the more nervous, Geoff Stokes or myself!

The Rainbow Melody Makers were beginning to look the part, with dark suits, white shirts, bow ties and music stands emblazoned with "RM", which we had bought from Farmers music shop in Wellington Street. We couldn't use this name outside the club, so it was decided to change – still using the 'RM'. Of the many big American bands, two were our particular favourites, Glenn Miller and Ray Anthony, so the band's new name would be Ray Miller.

As we progressed, we outgrew the arrangements that Ken had been doing so diligently from my piano copies, and he must have been relieved when we started buying professional band parts that were available as standard songs ("Golden

The Rainbow Melody Makers at Batford School, Pickford Hill, Harpenden, 25th January 1958. David Johns (Drums); Bob Rumbelow (Double Bass); Ken Tibbs (Tenor Sax); Michael Cooper (2nd Alto Sax); Ken Hendley (Lead Alto Sax); Brian Wiles (Trumpet); Yours Truly (Piano).

MODERN DANCES

SOCIALS

WEDDINGS

DINNERS etc.

All Catered For

THE RAY MILLER DANCE BAND

Secretary—
S. Goodyear
112 Walcot Avenue,
Luton, Beds.

Music for the connoisseur . . . .
by **RAY MILLER**
AND HIS ORCHESTRA

Modern Dances : Socials : Weddings : All catered for

Contact: **D. E. Johns, 89 Kingston Road, Luton**

THE LUTON BAND WITH THE LONDON REPUTATION

THE STUDENTS' UNION
Luton & South Beds. College of Further Education

Present an

END OF TERM DANCE

FRIDAY, JUNE 27th, 1958

in the

CRESTA SMALL BALLROOM, LUTON

· · · · · · · · ·

Non-Stop Music by
THE LEASIDE SIX and THE RAY MILLER BAND

8 — 12 p.m.   Ticket 3/-

Above left Our first band card for the newly named Ray Miller Dance Band – 1958.

Above right A 1959 advert (aiming upmarket) for Ray Miller and his Orchestra. Drummer David and I were sharing the mantle of managing the Band.

Left One of our first events as Ray Miller, shared with the ever popular Leaside Six.

Corn") or the latest 'pop' releases, the most popular being those arranged by Jimmy Lally. We started to build up a library, to include the dances of the day i.e. Quickstep, Foxtrot, Waltz, Tango, and Samba etc. The arrangements could be used by solo pianist through to 16-piece orchestra. We were buying one or two orchestrations each week in an effort to build up a good library as quickly as possible, from any one of the many music shops in the Oxford Street area of London. Eventually the band opened an account with Bron's music club, who ran an excellent postal service, and stocked a comprehensive choice of standard numbers, which was continually added to with the latest 'pop' numbers. All bands were using these arrangements and their familiarity helped the many musicians who freelanced between bands.

Our emerging regulars included Keith Indge (trumpet), Ken Hendley (alto sax), Mick Cooper (alto sax), Brian Fielder (trumpet) and Bob Rumbelow (bass player). Peter Tasker (tenor sax) was also a good friend and regularly came to rehearsals and took bookings with us at every opportunity. He was also responsible for making some extra music stands for us at his work, which was greatly appreciated.

Keith and Ken also worked at Napiers. Keith was a metallurgist in the laboratory, and Ken was Technical Publications Manager. Ken first joined us on Friday 12th July 1957 and Keith joined later, probably during 1958. Keith lived nearby in Stanford Road with his parents, and we became great drinking buddies at either the Somerset Tavern or Jolly Topers.

Keith remembers being up a ladder painting his parents' house when Dad and I first visited him, through recommendation, to play for us, shortly after he completed his national service in 1958. He is still playing lead trumpet with the Vauxhall Concert Band and a Hitchin Brass Ensemble – aged 65. During his two year national service, Keith was billeted with ex Luton Grammar School boy Graham Collier who was destined to become a most distinguished jazz musician and composer, receiving the highest accolades from every corner of the globe. Graham's career has been dedicated to the promotion of jazz in every aspect from performing and recording to lecturing and writing.

Ken Hendley had already secured himself a place in Luton's history, when in 1939 he became the first apprentice to be taken on by Percivals Aircraft factory at the town's airport – for which he had to pay! From there he joined the Voluntary Reserve when World war 11 was imminent and was one of the first to be called up into service with the R.A.F. in 1939. Already a pianist, he took up alto sax (and soprano) which he played throughout the war, alongside many famous musical servicemen, notably Cyril Stapleton, George Chisholm, Bob and Frank Cordell and Denny Dennis. Ken's greatest pride though, was being invited to play for The Squadronaires for several weeks, to cover for an injury to the regular band member.

Bob Rumbelow joined in the August of '57 and lived at Hitchin, but was getting work with other groups, and was soon to leave our 'merry band', which left us without a bass player.

How Mick Cooper from Harpenden ever made contact with us I cannot

Luton Grammar School boy, Graham Collier – son of Jack – was destined to be an internationally famous Jazz musician, and was billeted with Lutonian Keith Indge during his National Service call up.

remember, but he was also the nicest of people, totally reliable and, like us, keen to learn. Mick was with us for about 18 months but possibly found it hard going and bade farewell.

Now Brian Fielder <u>was</u> an old hand and technically excellent. His experience was unquestionable and, even though his brusque nature ruffled a few feathers, his knowledge and expertise nonetheless guided us through many 'sticky' rehearsals.

Going into 1958 we had a nice little outfit, with a reasonable amount of dance dates (generally referred to as 'gigs'), a good library, but still no bass player.

Dad was ever present and supportive, and he used to play accordion, double bass and violin with his own band before the (1939–45) war and had long since retired from the music scene, until now! Having played the bass, he volunteered to take it up again, with us, and before you knew it, he was to be the obvious 'stalwart' 4th player. The four of us were to be the backbone of the band, steering a progressive and steady course through our formative years, but unknowingly at the tail-end of the big band era with the new music of skiffle, trad/modern jazz and Rock & Roll about to take centre stage.

There was a downside though, because Dad had long since stopped driving, so as well as carrying the amplification, music, jackets and David with drum kit, I now had Dad <u>and</u> a double bass! The bass rested on top of the seats, with the neck pointing frontward, which was uncomfortable for all concerned, but it was the only way.

I enjoyed Dave's company after a gig, re-capping the night, and general lads chat, but Dad (bless him) was a real chatterbox after a few pints, so journeys home took on a new dimension. Whenever we travelled past Alec Sims hairdressing shop at 834 Dunstable Road (opp. Hayhurst Road), Dad always reminded us that Alec was his drummer before the (1939–45) war. I knew that Alec's son Paul continued with the business after his death in 1988, so a long overdue visit was called for, which turned out to be invaluable in respect of photographs, information, and a good deal of reminiscing with Paul.

Our car Vauxhall H type, ENM 777, earned its keep and was a good friend to the band in those early days, but we couldn't manage all the gear in the one car, so new member Keith Indge volunteered to pick up David and drums, from Kingston Road, in his SS Jaguar, which was a great help.

We were soon to find out that the problems which caused most aggravation were 'being let down'. The last minute phone call to 'cry off' an engagement was very annoying, which often meant sitting on the phone all day Saturday or running round houses right up to the 11th hour. This happened many times, but even worse was when a player just didn't turn up.

To Dad, who always tended to be the "worrier", these occurrences took the gloss off playing for him, because if it affected the band's performance: he took it personally, bearing in mind that, even if we managed to find a replacement, they very often did not come up to expectations, and you could bet your bottom dollar that if we had a bad night, there would be friends or relations present, or someone who had come to listen to you with the possibility of future bookings on offer. The band was still learning the trade, and in hindsight some of the bookings we should not have taken, but we learnt some hard lessons very quickly.

I can remember being asked to play a Samba at the T.U.C. Club in Church Street, Luton one evening, which was a request I shall never forget. I started too fast and, as panic set in, just got faster and faster. David just followed me on drums, not being too confident either! I don't remember there being any dancers left on the floor

BAR EXTENSION TO 12.30 a.m.

031

LATE TRANSPORT
COACH WILL LEAVE FROM CRESTA MAIN
ENTRANCE AT 1.05 a.m.

CHRISTMAS
DINNER
and
DANCE

15/6

3

THE CRESTA DOME BALLROOM
L U T O N

THURSDAY, 18th DECEMBER
1 9 5 8

ELECTRONICS DEPT., LUTON

DRESS INFORMAL

MENU

SOUP
ROAST CHICKEN
GRILLED TOMATOES
GARDEN PEAS
ROAST POTATOES
CREAMED POTATOES
CHRISTMAS PUDDING AND BRANDY SAUCE
COFFEE
CHEESE AND BISCUITS

DRINKS AVAILABLE TO INDIVIDUAL ORDER

PROGRAMME

7.45 p.m.   Dinner - Restaurant

9.00 p.m.   Dancing to the Ray Miller Band

10.30 p m.   Cabaret

11.00 p.m.   Dancing : Novelty Dances, Spot
Prizes

———

Auld Lang Syne
12.55 a.m.

ENGLISH ELECTRIC APPRENTICES ASSOCIATION
Present

A GRAND
CHRISTMAS DANCE
at the
WINTER ASSEMBLY HALL, LUTON
On FRIDAY 12th DECEMBER 1958
Dancing to
THE RAY MILLER DANCE BAND
8.00 p.m. to 12.00 Midnight   *BUFFET*

LICENSED BAR   149   NO JITTERBUGGING
TICKETS 3/6d.

Winter 1958, and we were
starting to get a steady
flow of seasonal bookings –
these two from our friends
at English Electric, Luton
Airport.

The Trade Union Club in Church Street, Luton (entrance opp. Parish Church) had a busy social calendar, and was very popular with club members and their families at the weekend. This is a typical scene, showing entertainment secretary Bob Hall on the mic. and the Freddie Wells Quartet, at an early 1950s club evening. Line up of band l. to r.: Bill Jones (Double Bass); Freddie Wells (Drums); Les Hyde (Alto Sax); Ron Hull (Piano).

at the end of the number! After that I rehearsed the Samba, and appreciated how relaxed the tempo is. From then on I grew to love Latin American music and became a skilled exponent.

The T.U.C. Club were very good to us and for a while we were almost resident, between our other bookings, thanks to the very friendly entertainment secretary Bob Hall.

Well there we were, playing our Jimmy Lally's, and using every booking as if it were a gala performance, whether it was at Beech Hill Conservative Club, The Town Hall, Assembly Room or a Village Hall. Some of the organisations that booked us certainly got more for their money than they had booked. But it paid off, as we were picking up the experience and the bookings. The occasional 'better' bookings came in and, although we were capable, we knew we would have to augment with one or two of the 'top' local musicians to give us the necessary punch, plus insurance against the unknown! Some of those guys who played with us in the early days became great friends and regular guests of the band for many years.

The band on stage, at the Trade Union Club, Church Street, Luton, 1958.
Line up l. to r.: Brian Fielder (Trumpet); David Johns (partly hidden) (Drums); Ken
Hendley (1st Alto Sax); Michael Cooper (2nd Alto Sax); Stuart Goodyear (Snr) (Double
Bass); Ken Tibbs (Tenor Saxophone); Stuart Goodyear (Jnr) Piano.

The small assembly room at the Luton Town Hall was a popular dance venue for privately-
booked functions. Here Jimmy Harrison's Trio is shown playing for the 'Blue Peter Club'
on 4th January 1968. Line up: Bruce Bonfield (Drums); Denny Cox (Double Bass); Jimmy
(Piano).

As a special friend, I mention with affection Islington born Mark Fischer, who, although at the time a member of the Ken Green Orchestra at The 'George', played with us and rehearsed at every opportunity. His experience played no small part in our rapid progress, whilst simultaneously introducing us into the 'circle' of the older and more experienced local musicians. He was also a great help during the compilation of these memoirs, and I visited him and Diane many times at their home in Anstee Road. Sadly he died in May 2001, just prior to another planned visit!

Some of the pianos we had to play on had seen better days, and were often well out of tune so, bearing in mind that every instrument would tune to the 'A' (above middle C) of the piano before playing commenced, tuning was often a lengthy exercise. Many of the 'old boys' must have seen it all before and, if the piano was really bad, they found it almost impossible to tune into it. They would get as near to it as possible and conclude by saying "It's good enough for jazz"!

I served on the Town Council for three years (1965–68) and tried to put the world to rights – at least the piano at the Town Hall! It was reported in the February 1966 issue of the Musicians' Union 'Tempo' Newsletter.

I used to hang on to all the amusing quips and anecdotes that the old boys used to come out with, for instance, during two waltzes that we played regularly, 'Someday I'll Find You', they would sing out (their own) second line "Creep up behind you"; and during the number, 'Always', sang out their own word, "sideways", so it became – "I'll be loving you – Sideways"!! So on and so forth.

Ken Green and his band (c.early 1960s), this time on duty at the Winter Assembly Hall. Line-up from top down: Ray Deakin (Trombone); Vernon Deakin (Trumpet); Ken Green (Trumpet, standing); Norman Wesley (Piano); Harry Kane (Alto Sax); Gordon Buckley (Alto Sax); Mark Fischer (Tenor Sax); Reg Harris (Tenor Sax); out of picture: Vince Shepherd (Baritone Sax) & Jerry Blain (Drums). The picture captures Mark Fischer, a good friend, with white handkerchief in top pocket, as I will always remember him.

Everybody smoked (and drank) on stage and passed cigarettes round between numbers. I can remember Mark placing a newly lit cigarette behind his ear or under the top note of his tenor, rather than put it out during the dance set.

It wasn't too long before I was contacted to play piano at some of the smaller venues locally and, as we were not yet getting dates as a band every weekend, the opportunity was there to earn a 'couple of quid' on a Saturday if I wished. (I wasn't earning much more than that for a whole week's work, as an apprentice!).

Dad pushed me into doing one at the Glen Eagle Hotel, Harpenden, which was a very smart Dinner/Dance venue and required music during dinner, then about an hour of music for dancing. It was a very lonely four hours, but, as Dad originally said "you'll have money in your pocket when all your mates would be broke", and of course he was right. Bernard Hemmings was the Maitre d'hôte and wanted me to fill the other dates when I was available. I <u>was</u> prepared to do more, so long as I could take a drummer also. This was agreed, and Johnny Walker or Laurie Pulleston made up the duo on many occasions. The diners were very good to us, and drinks flowed freely, especially when we played a request. Thank goodness there were no drink driving laws then. Bernard, who was tall, with black brylcreemed hair, and always immaculate in his evening jacket and grey striped trousers, motivated his staff with military precision by discreet and predefined well planned gestures.

I also played regularly in the lounge bar at the Three Horseshoes, Leagrave on Sundays, again with a drummer, which was very popular as a couples bar. The manager asked if I knew of a cabaret act to bring along, and just on the scene was trumpeter Eddie Houghton whom I had been using with the big band. In passing, he had mentioned his 'entertaining' expertise, so I booked him in. He was a natural, and played muted trumpet whilst walking round the tables, complete with silk handkerchief draped in his top pocket for special effect, which he used nonchalantly during his act. Eddie, an 'old pro' in every sense, milked the audience for requests, usually with a beverage reward, because a handkerchief was usually the only thing he ever took out of his pocket all night! This was my first experience at supporting cabaret.

Pictured in the Lounge Bar at the Three Horseshoes, Leagrave (now McDonalds Drive-Thru Restaurant) early 1950s are Jack Collier (Drums), Spence Bell (Piano) and Frank Pullen (Violin). Most of the larger Public Houses provided live weekend music.

I was soon to decline solo and duo work because I valued the time off, and it was very tiring, and it also meant booking a drummer just for the evening, as David didn't enjoy duo work either. A Sunday engagement (New Years Eve 1961) at the Trade Union Club, Church Street, was to be the one which dampened my brief flirtation with solo work. As a band we had been booked to play in the hall for dancing, but it had been snowing all day, and to journey by car would be impossible.

Wishing not to let them down, I towed my music and small amplifier from Walcot Avenue to the club on a sledge (and back home afterwards) and played for singing and dancing in the front bar, for a happy band of locals. Although 'double pay' of £3.00 was an obvious spur, it still took all my youthful exuberance to get me through the gig. It had been good grounding for me, as I was to play piano for the diners at hundreds of dinner dance functions with the band in the ensuing years.

Inevitably, I learned some numbers off by heart, such as 'Happy Birthday', 'Anniversary Waltz', 'We'll Meet Again', 'Wish Me Luck (as you wave me goodbye)', 'For he's/she's a jolly good fellow', 'Auld Lang Syne' and 'The National Anthem', for obvious reasons.

Exciting Times

Luton was a vibrant town, which provided high class live music for dancing on a weekly basis, to suit all tastes, and there are many stories to tell. So where do I start?

Accordion bands were very popular in the 1930s and 1940s and one such band, The Rhythmics, would have been typical of many, and was formed at Hitchin Road Youth Centre. They played regularly at Oxen Road Club and the Brewery Club, Park Street West. So take The Rhythmics, or similarly The 5 Aces, and you can visualise the entertainment of the day, and the guarantee was that it was <u>live</u>. Every cinema had a resident organist who would play during the interval on an organ that 'rose' up from the pit area, and on special occasions a band would be booked to play on the stage as well. So it was live music everywhere.

A selection of business cards for 1930s/40s Dance Bands.

'A Band Wagon' promoting the 1949 film "The Barkleys of Broadway" starring Fred Astaire & Ginger Rogers at the Savoy cinema, George Street, Luton, and Sunday Jazz at the Luton Jazz Club, 'Percivals Club', Castle Street. This was possibly to promote the new venue, as the Luton Jazz Club was previously held in Napiers Club on Park Square. Players: Back Four: Harry Lines (Baritone Sax); Syd Margolis (Drummer); Not known; Not known. Front Two: Harold Margolis (Clarinet); Stuart Horn (Tenor Sax).

The Five Aces Accordion Band (Disco of the day) at St Peters Hall, Dallow Road, Luton, c.1938 – Line-up: (back l–r) Johnny Green, Derek Hutchinson; (front l–r) Eric Ashby (Georges's Brother), John 'Jerry' Blain (Drums), Frank Blain – were typical of the young accordion bands of the 1930s.

The Blenheim Players shown here at St Andrews Church Hall, Luton (c.1935). The Band's first regular bookings were at the Busy Bee Café, Bury Park Road, 1935/36. Line-up: Gordon Harvey (Piano); Stuart Horn (Clarinet); Jack Hallam (Drums). Prior to the availability of amplification, it was commonplace for cards to be displayed, indicating the next dance. Note "Waltz" on piano!

Live on stage at the Savoy Cinema, George St. to promote the 1950 film 'Young Man with a Horn' starring Kirk Douglas were, l. to r.: Bill Harris (Piano); John Toomey-Wilson (Clarinet); Stuart Horn (Tenor Sax); Jerry Blain (Drums); Ray Deakin (Trombone); Jack Winch (Double Bass); Norman Willison (Trumpet). Exciting times indeed for cinema goers.

A typical crowd of the late 1930s in the Connaught Rooms. With bagpipes and kilts on view, New Years Eve or Caledonian Dance perhaps? The band in front row – suitably attired 1930s style – includes Bill Bates (Piano), Stuart Horn, with glasses, (Saxophone) and Harry Lines, extreme right, (Saxophone).

Sunday evening concerts at "The Union" cinema, Gordon Street were very popular. The local Tommy Thompson Trio is shown playing there in July 1941. The line up being: Jim Jeffries (Piano); Peter Brown (Cello); Tommy Thompson (Violin).
Intending to continue as an act in the profession was not to be. Peter and Jim were called up for wartime service in the R.A.F., but unfortunately neither survived.

Above The best bands were keen to enter the yearly round of the "Melody Maker" Band Competitions, not only for best band, but individual musicians' awards also. This (above left) was awarded as a band member of the winning band i.e. The Len Bolton Orchestra – 1945. The award (above right) was to Jerry Blain, who was adjudged to be the best drummer in the Championship.

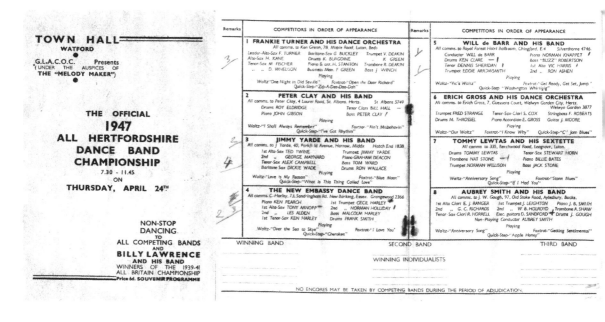

There were dozens of small bands in the 1940s and 50s to satisfy the requirements of a demanding public. There was no T.V. and, with radio still in its infancy, families were used to going out to be entertained. The local dance bands set a tremendously high standard, as they would have been compared to the big American and British Broadcasting Bands who were the equivalent of today's pop-stars. The rivalry between them was keen, and the very best would enter the annual regional dance band competitions run by the respected 'Melody Maker' music magazine, which would give the winning band tremendous prestige. Individual performances were also rewarded with a 'scroll' award.

Above On the bus, departing for Watford Town Hall and the 1946 Melody Maker Band Competition, is the Frankie Turner Dance Orchestra. Personnel of band: at rear, trombonist Ray Deakin; in front of him, wearing glasses, his brother Vernon Deakin (Trumpet); centre of picture, with glasses and scarf, Stuart Horn (Sax); front of picture, with bow tie, Jack Winch (Bass); extreme right, with moustache, Frank Turner; front, without bow tie, Eddie Burrell (band supporter).

Left Frankie Turner and Tommy Lewtas represented Luton at the Watford Town Hall 1947 Dance Band Championship. Tommy Lewtas hailed from Blackburn and quickly made his mark with Burton Gillis and also the Vauxhall Orchestra in the war time years. He went on to run his own band through the 1940s & 50s. Incidentally, drummer Freddie Wells taught Tommy's grandson David Perrins – and then David's son Daniel!

Jackie Morrison put a band together for the 1953 Melody Maker Band Competition, which was held at Oxford – and won! Picture shows winning line-up, and Jackie holding presentation trophy. Left to right: Eddie Hanson (Brass); name unknown but nicknamed 'Chang' (Trombone); Derek Impey (Bass); Bill Harris – with glasses (Piano); Bert Humphreys (1st Tenor Sax); Jerry Blain (Drums); Jackie Morrison (lead Alto Sax); Stuart Horn (2nd Alto); Mark Fischer (2nd Tenor). Judges with backs to camera.

Musicians were in plentiful supply, as many children were put on an instrument and taught by any one of a multitude of teachers. Ernest Congreve was an excellent tutor of stringed instruments, and not only gave individual tuition but also ran the Congreve Youth Orchestra from his Selbourne Road home. He was responsible for turning out many talented youngsters, particularly on violin and, although it wasn't to become their primary instrument in their later dance band days, Tommy Thompson, Alec Sims and Jimmy Harrison were three ex pupils who benefited from this thorough and dedicated tuition.

Apart from the larger town centre dance halls, other halls such as the Neville Hall in Neville Road, Limbury, The Drill Hall in Old Bedford Road and the All Saints Church Hall in Hampton Road, also ran regular weekly dances to meet a strong demand. Dancing was so popular, throughout the 1930s and 40s, that even the two roller skating rinks in Luton and Dunstable held regular weekend dances, which continued unabated through the '39–'45 war years into the 1950s. The skating rink in Luton was in Ramridge Road, Round Green, and called the Rola-Rink, where such bands as 'The New Victoria Players' would play for Friday night Ballroom Dancing, while The Half Moon Rink in London Road, Dunstable regularly had the Luton Accordion Dance Band or L. Brown and his band playing. The Half Moon Rink was called L'Europa in the 1950s.

Ernest Congreve (standing next to the piano) and his 'Congreves Junior Orchestra' pictured at the Edlesborough Garden Party & Fete, which was opened by Earl Brownlow, June 11th 1932.

1940s and still going strong, "The Congreves String Orchestra". (Tommy Thompson 2nd from left, front row).

Tommy McKenna and his Islanders, with supporting artistes, in Hawaiian mode, at the Icknield Halls, Letchworth 1948. Line-up l. to r.: Billy Lee (Trumpet); Ted Hounslow (Clarinet); Alec Sims (Drums); Bill _____ (Hawaiian guitar); Tommy McKenna (Guitar); Harold 'Schub' Stanton (Piano); unknown bass player. The Icknield Halls Building is still there, but is now used as offices.

Also, a whole variety of different and colourful bands were popular nationally; Troise (pro. Troys) and his Mandoliers was one of them, who topped the bill for a week at the Grand Theatre, Waller Street, in January 1940, and Britain's top accordion star, Tito Burns, played with his band at The George Hotel in March 1954.

Another, Felix Mendelssohn and his Hawaiian Serenaders, thrilled audiences on the radio and in the dance halls with his authentic sound of Hawaiian south sea music featuring the steel guitar. Fortunately for Luton, guitarist Tommy McKenna an ex-player with Felix, established his own band with the same distinctive Hawaiian sound, even down to the steel guitar, and made a big impact locally for many years.

Right Tommy McKenna's Band in carnival spirit once again at the Icknield Halls, Letchworth 1950. Line-up l.to r.: John Toomey-Wilson (Clarinet); Harry Hussey (Accordion); Ted Hounslow (Tenor Sax); Alec Sims (Drums); Tommy McKenna (Guitar); Bill Harris (Piano); (poss. Resilia Sports Club Christmas Dance, Wednesday 20th Dec 1950).

Tommy McKenna and his band at the Winter Assembly Hall, Luton, 1949. Tommy on guitar next to piano, and note the Hawaiian Steel guitarist next to him, for the authentic 'South Seas' sound.

I resurrected some old friendships and acquaintances along the way, who came up with a great deal of invaluable and detailed material. One of them was Bob Groom, with whom I worked at Vauxhall Motors for over 25 years; he reminded me of the many factories in Luton at this time who had their own bands and orchestras. As a teenager, he played clarinet in the Airport Orchestra (formed by D. Napier & Son) and the Luton Boys Club Band, then graduated into dance music and played alto saxophone for the Chris Wand Orchestra for many years. Other factory bands were George Kent's, the Vauxhall Orchestra (now the Vauxhall Concert Band),and the Davis Gas Stove Company's Orchestra (conducted by pianist Spence Bell), whose members also played for the town's many dance bands.

Early 1950s photo of the Vauxhall Apprentice Association Band. Only three can be positively identified: Dally Hughes (Drums); Bob Groom (Alto Sax); Roy Hammett (Accordion).

Opposite above The Airport Orchestra (formerly Napiers Orchestra) at rehearsals 1950/1. Note Vince Shepherd (Clarinet) with glasses, nurturing a young Bob Groom (Clarinet) extreme right. The venue is probably Napiers Club, which was above Hannibal Bonds shop on Park Square.

Opposite below Another 1950/1 shot of the Airport Orchestra rehearsing, this time exposing a young Billy Lee (Trumpet), in front of 'Exit' wearing glasses, who became a prominent dance band musician for many years.

John Coleman

Chairman

John took up the oboe as a youngster and played for the Artane School Orchestra, a well-known orchestra in Ireland. He also played with several bands and orchestras in Dublin and toured both Italy and France as a result. He had transferred to saxophone by the time he moved to Luton, and in the late 1950s he had his own 12-piece band at the old Cresta Ballroom. He joined Vauxhall as a metal polisher in January 1956 and by the end of that year was a member of the orchestra. He retired from Vauxhall in September 1986. John has been an active member continuously for the past 38 years, serving on the committee several times and chairing the band for the past two years. He met Vic Keach through the band and formed the 3-piece group 'Easitones'. They have played regularly at clubs, masonic functions and at dinner-dances for over 25 years — yet another example of music spreading from the Vauxhall Concert Band.

Keith Indge

Vice-Chairman

Keith's first contact with the orchestra was as a boy in 1949, when he used to have trumpet lessons with his uncle, Fred Green, just prior to the orchestral rehearsal. After his lesson he was allowed to sit next to Dick Kirk (1st trumpet) and follow the part he was playing. Later he joined the George Kent brass band and also became a member of the 'Blue Stars' dance band. His military service took him into the Green Howards in Hong Kong with Graham Collier — son of Jack Collier, Vauxhall Orchestra's drummer. After demob he played with the Airport Orchestra, which became the Luton Concert Orchestra, and also with the Ray Miller Orchestra at the California Ballroom. He gave up playing for 10 years due to dental problems, but eventually came back to the Vauxhall Motors Orchestra in 1973. He has been our solo trumpet ever since.

Biographical details of John Coleman (Chairman) and Keith Indge (Vice-Chairman) of the Vauxhall Concert Band, which were extracted from the Band's 'Diamond Jubilee Concert' programme at the Queensway Hall, Dunstable, on April 9th 1994. Both were stalwarts of the local music scene for many years.

Another Pair of Musicians

Jack Collier and Betty Dunkley

THESE occasional pictures and little write-ups about members of our Band have been appearing for some time now, but then our total complement of playing members is over 30.

This month we feature Jack Collier, drummer, and another lady, Betty Dunkley, who performs upon the fiddle.

JACK COLLIER

Jack was asked if he would supply a few notes of his own and the autobiography turned out so well that we publish it here without alteration or comment :

"Having annoyed parents for years rattling spoons, knives, and so on, decided to take up Drumming seriously.

"Joined Whitley Bay Orchestral Society and deputised for various cinema and theatre drummers.

"Took up profession in 1925 at South Shields as Drummer and Effects man, and derived great fun making silent films noisy. Played at other cinemas at Whitley Bay and on Tyneside, till the 'Yanks' invaded with their talkies ; I retreated three times to different cinemas whilst this was happening.

"After assisting local symphonic and orchestral societies, I decided to come to London as a painter. My work at Barking Power Station with a 4-inch brush caught the eye of my foreman, who sent me to the Vauxhall, where, he said, the chaps were 'too busy making bonus to notice any splashing !'

"Hearing of a new band being formed at Grand Theatre, I applied, gave audition, paid 6d. for contract stamp, and met Maestro Fred Green. Now we have had four happy years together.

"Have assisted most orchestras in Luton, also St. Albans Operatic Society."

You can tell that he enjoys life, can't you ?

BETTY DUNKLEY

Betty appears to have been almost an infant prodigy (like Shirley Temple, in a different sphere !). She started playing at Hillbrook School of Music, Tooting (if you know where that is), at the age of 7.

On reaching maturer years, she came to Harpenden, where she spent two years with the Bramblewick Junior Band, subsequently joining the Arden Light Orchestra, with which she stayed another four years.

Our own band received her in January, 1940, and since then Betty has been a regular and consistently cheerful member of an always enjoyable crowd.

Both she and Jack Collier say that they couldn't wish for a better lot of folk to work amongst.

Taken from the August 1941 issue of the Vauxhall Mirror, a biography of two members of the band. During the 1939–45 War, the band gave lunchtime concerts in the main canteen.

The Vauxhall Orchestra had the benefit of being able to play in the huge works canteen in Kimpton Road, and during the 1939–45 war gave lunch time concerts to the workers, and very often had 'top stars' as guests on the show. Violinist Gilbert Pinder played with the Orchestra when he joined Vauxhall in the mid 1930s, having left his native Halifax, where he also played for the 'Mackintosh's Toffee' factory orchestra. His outstanding memory of the Vauxhall lunchtime concerts was meeting the piano stars Rawicz and Landauer and guiding them into the canteen – where, having entered, they remarked "Blimey, St. Pancras Station"!

Above All eyes are on the famous B.B.C. commentator and announcer Alvar Liddell at a 'Workers Playtime' concert held in the Vauxhall Motors main works canteen (c.1941). Conducting The Vauxhall Orchestra is Fred Green, and the two attentive vocalists are Frances Turner (extreme left) and Barbara Bird.

Left Recording stars Rawicz & Landauer gave a concert with the Vauxhall Orchestra in the main works canteen.

Right Taking time out, at the 'Workers Playtime' concert, l. to r.: Norman Bradley, Frances Turner, Herbert Morrison M.P., Barbara Bird, Fred Green.

Above Herbert Morrison M.P. addressing his Vauxhall audience during a 'Workers Playtime' concert in the main works canteen, Kimpton Road (c.1941). Herbert Morrison was Minister of Supply briefly in 1940, before becoming Home Secretary and Minister for Home Security 1940–45, in the War Time Cabinet.
Below Vocalists, l.to r.: Norman Bradley, Frances Turner & Barbara Bird, together with pianist Jack Yeomans and leader Fred Green, front the Vauxhall Orchestra.

The Luton Boys Club Band c.1950. Line-up: Ray 'Fluff' Franklin (Piano); Johnny O'Carroll (Double Bass); Eddie Childs (Drums); Jimmy Marsh (Trumpet); Bill ——— (Trombone); John Lambert (Tenor Sax); Pete Jeffs (Tenor Sax); Bob Groom (Clarinet); Don Barrett (Alto Sax).

Boys Clubs were numerous around the town and well supported, and the dedication of the club leaders who ran them resulted in 'many a boy' finding a vocation on an instrument. John Wilson was one such club leader at the Luton Boys Club, on the corner of Park Street and Chobham Street, (building still there) who had several instruments and formed a band from his enthusiastic boys. It was typical of many and a valuable springboard for the budding bandsmen into the local music scene. John Wilson left to work in Bermuda at the Headquarters of the National Association of Boys Clubs and unfortunately the band folded with his departure. Three other lads who also passed through the Boys Club band were Jimmy Marsh (trumpet), Don Barrett (alto saxophone), and Johnny O'Carroll (double bass) who all went on to make a big impact on the local dance scene in ensuing years. Jimmy was responsible for Johnnie owning his first double bass, when he saw a second hand one in the old Luton market for £7, which Johnny promptly purchased.

The Alma Theatre (corner of Alma and Manchester Street now Cresta House) became a cinema from Monday to Saturday and a concert theatre on Sundays. Concerts at the Alma had become an institution since the 1930s, where so many of the country's top performers played to packed houses. One of the most popular dance bands of all time, Joe Loss, played there on December 4th 1949. The Eric Winstone and Oscar Rabin bands also played there.

Denbigh Road Boys School Orchestra 1951. Conductor: Gilbert Pinnock. Others to be identified: John Murray (Violin/Leader) – front circle with glasses, sleeve rolled up; Peter Harrison (Saxophone); Kenny Boyes (Trumpet) – extreme right of Trumpets.

The Alma Theatre (seen here in the late 1940s) was to become a theatre/cinema, then a ballroom, and finally the Cresta Ballroom. The Co-operative Bank now occupies this site. (Bone & Co Music Shop, extreme right of picture).

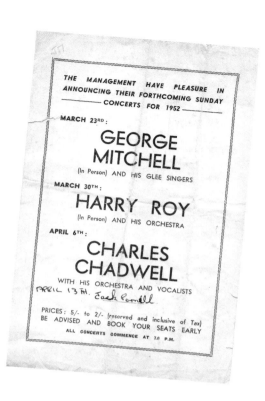

Alma Theatre programme 1952. On this occasion featuring Eric Winstone and his Orchestra. Forthcoming announcements highlighted quality of Sunday concerts.

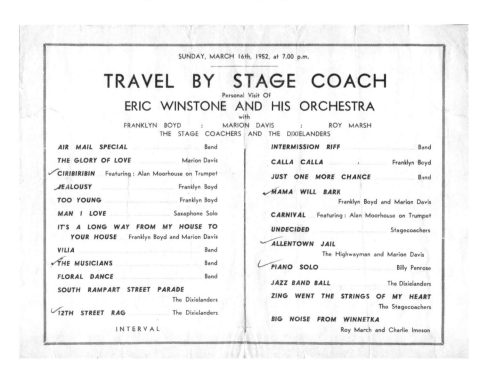

The Alma Theatre was host to a multitude of talents, and here, Ken Haywood on the
musical saw is supported by Sonny Goodyear on vocals and sax. (Ken Haywood was blind
or partially blind) (c.1940s).

Ken Green and his Orchestra on duty at a Sunday concert, at the Alma Theatre. Let the
show commence!

Spence Bells Band playing in the upstairs ballroom at the Alma, 1947. Line-up l. to r.: Fred Boutwood (Drums); Stuart Horn (Tenor Sax); Spence Bell (Piano); Harry Lines (Alto Sax/ Baritone Sax/ Clarinet). Note the ex-Vauxhall Orchestra music stands i.e. front grille design of Vauxhall Motor Car, with "V.M." replaced by musical notes "F.G.B." (Perhaps the booking was Fred G Boutwood's on this occasion!)

The ballroom upstairs (The Horseshoe Room) held public dances on Saturdays, and was available for private bookings on other nights, and weekend weddings etc. The last band to give a Sunday concert at the Alma was Ronnie Scott and his Orchestra on Sunday 11th July 1954, for it then closed on 17th July 1954, before re-opening as a Ballroom in early 1955.

The most popular local dance halls of the 1950s were The George Hotel, with resident band Ken Green; Harpenden Public Hall, where the very popular Geoff Stokes was considered resident, and the Cresta (The old Alma theatre/ cinema) with resident Don Smith, whose band was fully professional. His band was first class and it was no surprise when he landed a 'plum' residency at the Newcastle Oxford Galleries in 1958. He employed local double bass player Johnny O'Carroll in the band, who turned professional when he was offered full time employment with Don at Newcastle. The last full time professional band to play at the Cresta was Roy Kenton, who only did one winter season before leaving for a summer season elsewhere.

Right Don Smith and his Orchestra after he had left Luton, playing for BBC's "Come Dancing" at the Plaza Ballroom, Tynemouth, early 1960s. He was resident at Newcastle's Oxford Galleries, but the ceilings were not high enough to allow the cameras to cover sequence dancing, so transmission was transferred to the Plaza at nearby Tynemouth. Luton's Johnny O'Carroll is seen here on the Double Bass.

George Street, Luton, showing the George Hotel in 1936, by local artist Doug Jones.
Donated to me by Doug, for use in my book, this watercolour beautifully creates a tranquil
Luton.

Roy Kenton and his Band went to Ramsgate after vacating the residency at Luton's Cresta Ballroom, and are seen here at the Coronation Ballroom, Ramsgate, 1959.

Ken Tibbs and I decided on Ramsgate again for our summer holiday in 1959, having been there also in 1958, and who was playing at the Coronation Ballroom, none other than Roy Kenton and his orchestra! We had a great fortnight, became very friendly with the band, and on top of that, Ken met Betty at the Ballroom, and she was to become Mrs. Tibbs a year later on Saturday 15th October 1960 – I was Ken's Best Man.

The Luton Council converted Waller Street indoor swimming pool in the winter months for use as a dance hall etc., which they called the Winter Assembly Hall. The local bands keenly competed for the Saturday dates that the council invited them to tender for. Other evenings were allocated for private bookings, and my brother-in-law Hadyn Cook recalls a midweek function in December 1954 when the great Ted Heath was booked there for a dance. His singers Lita Roza and Dennis Lotis (who were themselves 'pop' stars) were also on stage, and Hadyn's mates bet him he couldn't persuade Lita off stage for a dance. With the help of a few pints, he approached the stage and asked Lita for a dance; she duly obliged, but had to return to the stage before the number finished, as she was singing the next one. So there you are, Lita did a song (and dance routine) in Luton! Ironically another close friend, David White, vividly recalled this dance, because for whatever reason, the band turned up in dribs and drabs, and started playing first as a quartet, then an octet etc. until eventually the whole band were on duty, to tumultuous applause.

Waller Street Baths, Luton, 1969.

Above The Waller Sreet Baths, which during the winter months was converted into the
Winter Assembly Hall by the Luton Council.
Below A typical dance night at the Winter Assembly Hall, Waller street (c.1945), with the
Frank Turner Band on stage.

A lady pianist at the Winter Assembly Hall, with the Maurice Edwards Band in 1958,
Yvonne Barrett was one of the few female instrumentalists on the scene. Line-up: to rear:
George Wallace (Drums); Lou Ferraro (Double Bass); Yvonne Barrett (Don's Sister)
(Piano); front Line: Jackie Morrison (Tenor Sax); Don Barrett (Alto Sax); Brian Sapwell
(Trumpet); Ray Deakin (Trombone); George Smith (M.C.).

Although he wasn't a regular attendee of Sunday concerts at the Alma, Hadyn just had to go when The Johnny Dankworth Seven featuring vocalist Cleo Laine played there. After an excellent evening, he sat for a while to unwind and by the time he got out to Alma St., Johnny, Cleo and the Band were making their exit also. He spoke at some length to Johnny and Cleo who were on a motorbike, and the rest of the band were in a van they had been loading. They said they lived at Watford and, when the van was packed, they rode off into the sunset, with Hadyn waving!!

Cleo Laine singing with the Johnny Dankworth Orchestra, January 1957. Although this picture was taken at the Queens Hall, Preston it is representative of them in the early days. (By kind permission of Dankworth Management).

Left Geoff Stokes and his band at the Winter Assembly Hall (c. mid 1950s). Line-up: back row (l. to r.): Jim Bull (Trumpet); Brian Sapwell (Trumpet); Keith Burgoine (Drums); Johnny O'Carroll (Double Bass); front line (l. to r.): Eric Slaney (Tenor Sax); Bob Stokes (Tenor Sax); Cecil Capon (Alto Sax); Geoff Stokes (Alto Sax); Bob Smith (Guitar); Harold 'Schub' Stanton (Piano).

The one and only Stan Kenton, seen here on the piano at the Cresta, when he appeared there with his band in 1956.

I can remember Ken Mackintosh and his band at the Cresta, who was a top 'palais'* performer throughout the country, and the great American Stan Kenton and his band also playing there, giving a matinee and evening performance on Tuesday March 13th 1956.

Hadyn's final recollection by a remarkable coincidence tied in with a story relayed to me (later on) by drummer Jerry Blain. Premier Drums sponsored a sales presentation of their drum kits in the small assembly room at Luton Town Hall and featured the top drummer Jack Parnell and musicians in October 1953. During his performance the bass drum kept 'creeping away' from him (on the polished stage), so he drove a nail into the stage, which did the trick, except the caretaker went wild! Local drummers were then invited to have a go, and who was one of them? Yes, Jerry.

One of my 'cousins' (on Mum's side) Peter Thompson from Harpenden, or 'Wor Peeta' as he was affectionately known, was making it big in 1957 with his Skiffle group The Vampires, and they even played at the Café De Paris, London. Although our music never brought us together commercially, I do remember a super family night at the Gosforth Park Hotel (in the Gosforth Park Race Track, Newcastle) where we played for a rare Geordie family get together.

Skiffle and Trad. Jazz were hugely popular from the late 1950s to the early 60s, and Peter was on hand to fill the huge local demand for Skiffle, and has kindly written a chapter for this book, recollecting those days, called Jazz, Skiffle and Rock & Roll.

*palais (palais de dance) was the name given to top dance halls.

The Leaside Six
present
THE STODGEHOUSE REUNION
at the
CRESTA DOME BALLROOM
on
FRIDAY, 26th SEPTEMBER, 1958 at 7.30 p.m.

Admission 3/6d   Refreshments

Left Typical dance ticket at
Early Trad. Dance.
Right Masks optional at this
1958 rave.

Presenting
'Un Bal Masqué' Rave
at
St. Mary's Hall
on
Friday, 7th November, 1958
7.30—11.45 p.m.
Music by Leaside Six
Refreshments   -   Masks Optional   -   Ticket 3/-
IN AID OF CHESHIRE HOMES

A weekly Trad Jazz evening was held on Wednesdays in the newly opened Cresta Ballroom, which featured the popular bands of the day such as Ken Colyer, Graham Bell and Chris Barber featuring Lonnie Donegan. Although well supported, the hall was too large for the right atmosphere.

Drummer Chris Morris and trumpeter Steve Mason formed the Luton Jazz Band, primarily to perform for Luton on the popular radio series Top Town in 1956 (which was produced by Barney Colehan), together with Vernon Critten Jnr (d/bass); Ray Sills (piano); Harold Fineberg (clarinet); Derek Richardson (trombone); Charlie McNamara (soprano sax); and Dave Martin (banjo). Having formed, they played in the small upstairs ballroom as the Delta Jazz Band, again on Wednesdays, with great success. This resulted in the opening of a Sunday club for members only, owing to licensing laws.

1958 handbills promoting the Delta Jazz Club, where local bands shared the billing with top touring outfits.

The Chris Morris Quartet (c.1959). L to r: Chris Morris (Drums); Rex Woodley (Double Bass); Harold Margolis (Clarinet/Tenor Sax); Keith Mayles (Piano). Harold Margolis was one of two musical brothers, the other being Syd, who played drums with all the top local bands.

There was so much material and detail to talk about, and talking to Chris Morris on Thursday 21st March '02 and Brian Sapwell on Friday 22nd March '02 was to be no exception. Luton born Chris is an internationally famous T.V. news presenter and took time out to visit my home, complete with his memories and photos. He went to the Abbey School, St. Albans, where he was taught the bugle, but then progressed onto drums, and eventually bought Eric May's 'Premier' drum kit for £50, paying it off at £1 per week, without telling his Dad. Chris was able to enlarge on my knowledge of the Alma, as that was where he spent much of his earlier days working on the opposite corner as a junior reporter on the 'Luton News', and as the drummer with his Delta Jazz Band in the small upstairs ballroom.

Chris Morris Band at Pirton Village Hall (early 1960s). L. to r.: unknown (Vibraphone); Keith Mayles (Piano); Mick Stone (Double Bass); Chris Morris (Drums); Ken Hendley (Alto Sax); Stuart Horn (Sax/Clarinet).Unfortunately, I could not recall or trace the 'Vibes' player, who I remember as being an excellent exponent of this very melodic but uncommon instrument.

The Alma and, opposite, the old Luton News Offices in Manchester Street, 1932. Donated for use in my book by local artist Doug Jones.

Some typically memorable dates are as follows:

16th April 1950	Alma Theatre Sunday Concert Ted Heath And His Music.
April 1955	Refurbishment of Alma Theatre complete. Opened as Alma Ballroom, with Vic Abbott and his Orchestra holding residency.
August 1955	Vic's residency concluded. Watford bandleader Eddy Clayton takes over.
Friday Nov 18th 1955	Hall now owned by Harold Davison Organisation and renamed the Cresta. Grand opening by 'Sabrina' and special guest Paul Carpenter as M/C compere, with the newly appointed band being Ronnie Pleydell and Jill Kinley on vocals.
January 27th 1956	Guest appearance of the Eric Delaney Band (Broke foot pedals during performance).
Wed 11th April 1956	From Wimbledon Palais, Don Smith Orchestra commences, with vocalist Shirley Wilson, for 2 year residency.
Friday 8th June 1956	Ted Heath and His Music, featuring vocalists Toni Eden, Bobbie Britton and Peter Lowe.
Tues 13th Nov 1956	Lionel Hampton and his Orchestra. A legendary Vibraphonist – died New York, August 31st 2002, aged 94.
April 1957	Ted Heath – 3rd visit to the Cresta Ballroom.
Sat 4th Jan 1958	Ted Heath and His Music.
Sat 1st February 1958	Ivy Benson and her Band.
1958–1959	Alan Clarke Orchestra takes on residency, followed by Roy Kenton.
9th January 1959	Humphrey Lyttelton and his band play in small upstairs 'Dome' Ballroom
31st January 1959	Lou Preager's 'Find the Singer' contest – Eric Mack and His Music.

In the Cresta Small Ballroom upstairs, drummer Pete Sims opened the Premier Jazz Club on Tuesday January 29th 1957, with Bill Harris (piano) and Jack Stone (d/bass) in support, as house band. The opening night guests were Tubby Hayes and Phil Bates. After a declining run it unfortunately closed in March '57.

The 7th Luton Company Boys Brigade Band, setting off from Stopsley 1943. Trumpeter Brian Sapwell is in there. Such bands were responsible for many youngsters' well-being, and music tuition, and became the ideal breeding ground for future musicians.

The evening with trumpeter Brian Sapwell in the Kings Arm's, Houghton Regis was a real pleasure, and tales of the old days flowed out as quick as the ale flowed down. He spoke with affection of his days in the Boys Brigade, where so many youngsters learned their instrument, and later in the RAF, where he played with other talented musicians from all over the country.

Luton Battalion Band marching in front of the New Barnet Brass Band, entering Chapel Street from Stuart Street. c.1943.

Many musicians soon found themselves 'in the band' when they did their National Service. This photo, typical of so many, shows Lutonian Peter Green on drums, in the R.A.F Watnall Band of 1951

Other local bands of that time were Don Cleaver (drummer); Benny Kidman; Tommy Thompson; Freddie Maydwell; The Debonaires; The Regency Dance Band; Jimmy Harrison; Ron Horrell & His Band; Al Morgan Trio; The Beverley Players; The Chris Rogers Orchestra (Managed by Brian Arnall, tenor sax); The Embassy Band; Jimmy Bland; Chris Wand and his Ballroom Orchestra; The Freddie Arnold Five; The Mayfair Players and the Carlton Orchestra. Chris Wand's orchestra was managed by a well-known local agent / M.C. Les Vass. Also, drummer Basil Osman ran the Barry Austyn Orchestra, with Stan Tisbury as tenor sax/arranger.

Left Derrick Smith later became a children's entertainer and opened a music shop in Wellington Street c.1969.

Right The Bedford based Freddie Maydwell Orchestra at Hitchin Town Hall in 1964, with vocalist Bette Lee in full song.

George Smith was a well known booking agent for local bands, and was also responsible for managing his own ensembles. Accordion bands were very popular just before and during the 1939–45 War, and here George is pictured (extreme right) with one of them. George was obviously responsible for this booking, with his son Derrick extreme left. The lady pianist and others unfortunately unknown.

DANCE BANDS

Ajax Trio/Quartet
E. Monk, 279 Chesford Road, Luton.
Ray Allan and His Music
R. T. Lelliot, 173 Dallow Road, Luton (1963).
The Apollo Trio
B. Bonfield, 36 Moor Street, Luton.
Freddy Arnold Band
F. Arnold, 271 Runley Road, Luton.
The Bandits Dance Band
B. Osman, 40 Knoll Rise, Luton (2974).
The Dave Carlton Orchestra
D. B. Morris, 612 Dunstable Road, Luton (2676-day; 51310-evening).
John Collier Trio
J. Collier, 50 Derwent Road, Luton.
Ken Green and His Orchestra
F. W. Green, 1 Clifton Road, Luton (6096).
Jimmy Harrison Trio/Quartet
J. Harrison, 47 Vincent Road, Luton (52147).
The Everett Peterson Trio
P. E. Green, 193 Barton Road, Luton (Icknield 587).
Stan Lee and His Band
S. Tisbury, 1 Honeygate, Luton (8288).
The Luton Jazz Band
C. H. Morris, The Old Hall, Pirton, Herts. (Pirton 275).
The Leaside Seven
R. H. Bates, 167 Ashburnham Road, Luton.
The Royal Garden Seven
G. J. Vickers, 20 Hillfield Avenue, Hitchin (Hitchin 3476).
Roy Marsh Trio/Quartet
R. M. Marsh, 55a Gardenia Avenue, Luton (53162).
Freddie Maydwell and His Orchestra
F. Maydwell, 'Trescoe', South Avenue, Elstow, Bedford (Bedford 5613).

Tommy McKenna and His Music
T. McKenna, 2 Redferns Close, Luton (7184).
Ray Miller Orchestra
S. J. Goodyear, 112 Walcot Avenue, Luton.
John Scott Band
J. P. Scott, 498 Dunstable Road, Luton (51992).
Geoff Stokes Orchestra
George Smith, 49 Grantham Road, Luton (52573).
Tommy Thompson Orchestra
L. A. Vass, 38 Newcombe Road, Luton (5128).
Savannah City Jazz Band
M. D. Facer, 500 Hitchin Road, Luton.
The Roy Stevens Jazzmen
S. Mason, 'Sunnybank', Catsbrook Road, Luton (Icknield 688).

A selection of local dance bands from the late 1950s.

The Barry Austyn Orchestra at the Dunstable Queensway Hall (late 1960s). Leader Basil Osman is resplendent in a white coat with a carnation buttonhole. Basil is conducting – complete with baton – and the line up is: rhythm: Ron Franks (Piano); Don Howarth (Double Bass); Kenny Gorrell (Drums). Saxes l. to r.: John Murray (Alto Sax); Denis Kensit (Alto Sax); Stan Tisbury (Tenor Sax); Don Barrett (Tenor Sax). Brass (not in picture): Terry Hext (Trombone); Brian Sapwell (Trumpet); George Ashby (Trumpet). Watford-based Gordon Rushton was also regularly booked as the trombonist with the band.

These bands were competing for the pick of the many private functions, and we must not forget Old Tyme Dances, which were still popular, where you would dance The Veleta, The Military Two Step and the Gay Gordons etc. Either Cecil Arnold's Band, Billy Lawrence and his Orchestra or Jimmy Harrison would excel at these functions, with Jimmy occasionally using a violin lead of either Peter Bennett or Dave Bell, the son of pianist Spence Bell.

Electrolux Apprentices run 50/50 Dance in their canteen.

Occasionally we would pick up a 50/50 dance evening, where half of the dances were Old Tyme and half Modern.

Joe Lovesey and his Orchestra from Wolverton were also a very professional Old Tyme outfit during the 1940s and 50s, and regularly played at SKF, Vauxhall Motors and Bedford Corn Exchange with a 12 or 14 piece orchestra.

A 1940s dance at the Winter Assembly Hall, with the dancers in formation doing the barn dance or Gay Gordons perhaps!!

"Take your partners for old tyme." Joe Lovesey & his Orchestra.

An impromptu session, at a Monday evening Bagshawe's Jazz Evening c.1959. From back, left to right: Tony Broughall (Drums); Alan Higgs (Maracas); David Bradley (Tambourine); Les Wood (with Drumsticks); front on Bongoes, Freddie Wells; Double Bass Player (out of picture), Rex Woodley.

Monday nights were a good night to go out and re-cap on the weekend, and where better than Bagshawe's factory social club at Dunstable (opp. First & Last P.H.), where some of the most talented exponents of modern jazz would show off their talents to the delight of an enthusiastic audience. Each session was totally unrehearsed, and the musicians who dropped in gave their services for the pure enjoyment they received. Some of those who played regularly I remember well: Philip 'Pip' Hallman (d/bass); Stuart Horn (alto sax/piano); Bill Harris (piano); Dally Hughes (drums); Freddie Wells (drums); Eric May (drums); Alan Higgs (drums); Rex Woodley (d/bass); Dave Bradley (sax); Tony Broughall (drums); John Wallwork (guitar) and a special friend Les Wood (drums). The most unforgettable night was undoubtedly when the great tenor saxophonist Don Rendell made a guest appearance.

The Bill Harris Trio at the USAF Chicksands. Keith Burgoine (Drums); Jackie Morrison (Alto Sax); Bill Harris (Piano); plus Geoff Fullelove (Double Bass), American Serviceman at base, who also sang like Nat 'King' Cole. The United States Air Force Base at Chicksands (Nr Shefford) called upon local musicians to provide bands for their many social functions.

Opposite above Monday 29th February 1960, at Bagshawe's Jazz Evening, saw top saxophonist Don Rendell make a guest apperance. He was supported by regulars Bill Harris (Piano), Alan Higgs (Drums), John 'Wally' Wallwork (Guitar) and Stuart Horn (Sax). Don is seen here playing with Bill Harris on piano and Stuart Horn standing between them. An appreciative audience coincidentally includes my future wife Margaret, extreme right of the 3 girls (I did not know her at this time), Mick Stone (arms folded) and drummer George Wallace (holding bottle).

Opposite below Interval time at Bagshawe's – with some of the regulars, l. to r.: Rex Woodley (sitting on his Double Bass); Stuart Horn; Mary Woodley; Pat Ayres; Les Wood (sitting on case); Charlie Goss (standing).

Stuart Horn (left) & Jackie Morrison (right), two
of the best modern jazz exponents from Luton –
playing together on alto saxophones.

Les and Stuart ran the busy Les Stuart Trio, who were also resident at the Luton Social Working Men's Club & Institute, Smith's Lane on Sundays. Lutonian Stuart Horn was a very versatile and accomplished musician and during his career played for just about every band in the area, on either piano, alto saxophone or tenor saxophone.

It was good to visit Stuart, in February 2002, at his Bishopscote Road bungalow, and at 81 years old, he was still keen to reflect on the old days and browse through his photo albums. It turned out that he had the same pianoforte teacher as myself – May Gough. Stuart died on 2nd June 2002.

Modern jazz was the new phenomenon and was rapidly gaining in popularity, but, because of the intricacies of its execution, not too many musicians took to playing it. In general, the melody would be played to get into the number, then each instrument would improvise on the theme in turn, then they would all join in for the last chorus, returning to the melody. Modern jazz never became hugely popular because to 'get into it' you needed an understanding of music. From the late 1950s through into the early 60s the club ran with a great 'smokey' atmosphere, and low lights, where it was eyes closed and heads nodding to the rhythm – and that was the audience!

The fashions of the day would dictate, to a degree, the way you danced, and this partially fell into two camps, The Mods and The Rockers. The male Mods with their winkle picker shoes, smart suits with taper trousers and short jackets, slim ties and short haircuts, tended to act 'suave' and would dance accordingly. Their preferred music would be in the modern jazz idiom. If they bought transport it tended to be a scooter.

Right A Jazz session at the Luton Industrial Mission, Chapel Street, 1968. On duty l. to r.: Trevor Evans (Piano); Jim Douglas (Guitar) hidden; Kenny Gorrell (Drums); Denny Cox (Bass). (Pianist Trevor Evans not to be confused with local bass player of the same name!) Trevor, on piano, met his wife-to-be Breada, at this function.

Another 'Mod' taking the floor, (now who could that be???) and the young lady long forgotten I'm afraid! Dancing was always on tap, even at darts finals. (During 1961, I was seconded to work at the U.K.A.E., Harwell, Berks., by D. Napier & Son at Luton Airport).

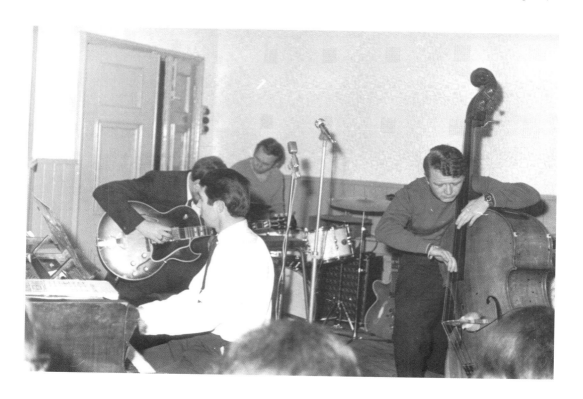

Rockers covered a broader base. Those who rode motor cycles wore leathers and jeans, heavy boots and were also known as greasers, but didn't venture near a dance floor very often. But the lads who propelled themselves into the fashion spotlight as dedicated followers of the latest dance craze of Rock and Roll were undoubtedly the Teddy Boys. They wore long jackets (often with velvet collars), drainpipe trousers, thick sole suede shoes, and their hair would be 'Brylcreemed' in the Elvis Presley or Tony Curtis style. The Mods and Teddy Boys did go dancing, but would only dance in the style that suited them, but there was still a hardcore of middle of the road youngsters (squares) who could be depended on to foxtrot or waltz etc.

New Years Eve Dance ticket at the
Cresta Dome Ballroom (c.1958)
with the Leaside Six.

One must not forget the followers of traditional jazz, where the girls and boys dressed similarly in sloppy sweaters and duffel coats and tended to sport long hair, and jived to every number 'with enthusiasm'. They (and the Mods) were soon to fade away, but the Rockers and Teddy Boys became established for many years. They seemed to stay in prominence more so in the country districts and from the late 1950s right through the 1970s would attend Working Men's Social Clubs at weekends in large numbers. We regarded Tring, Leighton Buzzard, Bletchley and Biggleswade as the 'Rocking Belt' where we would have to play Rock and Roll all night. We tried to avoid these bookings, which were better left to the Rock Groups.

The demand for bands (and groups) was considerable up to the mid 1960s, when every function, such as weddings, anniversaries, street parties, office dos etc., would have had live music. Discos then became very popular, especially with the younger generation, and were soon to be the 'norm' at many functions.

Left All functions would book live music for their entertainment and dancing. The Billy Seaford Trio are pictured here enjoying what appears to be a private function. Pianist Billy is accompanied by Keith Burgoine (Drums) and Dennis Tilcock (Double Bass).

Members of the Vauxhall Orchestra entertain patients and staff on Christmas Day at St
Marys Hospital, Luton (early 1940s). Fred Green (with baton); Barbara Bird; Frances
Turner; Jack Yeomans (Piano); Ken Smith (m.c./compere) with moustache; Jack Collier
(Drummer) behind him; Jimmy Chappin (props/scenery etc) extreme rear corner of room;
his wife Winifred on accordion.

Accordion players were in demand to provide music at outdoor parties. Jimmy Harrison
was the Accordionist booked for this Rotarians' 1950s Bonfire Night (poss. Woodside Farm,
Nr. Luton).

104-115 DIVS.

BUFFET DANCE

AT AL CANTEEN - RED ROOM
ON SATURDAY OCTOBER 9th. 1971
8 p.m. - midnight

Dancing to Ray Miller and his Band

TICKETS 80p   Bar 8 - 11 p.m.

V.M.R.C. **DUNSTABLE**
D4 Social Club

present a
Buffet Dance
In The Main Dining Hall, Boscombe Road,
Saturday. 4th December, 1982
Dancing 8-00 p.m. to Midnight Music by The
Ray Miller Dance Band

Tickets £3·50 Each.
Rights Of Admission Reserved.

**There were always lots of week-end functions at the Vauxhall Luton & Dunstable Plants.
Notice the price difference for buffet dance between 1971 and 1982. The AL canteen was in
Osborne Rd, Luton.**

On top of this, all the factories in town had busy social calendars, and in particular Vauxhall (Luton), Bedford Trucks (Dunstable), Electrolux (Luton), AC Delco (Dunstable) and the Vauxhall Parts Dept. (Toddington Road) were always running weekend dances, which allowed public access. The Vauxhall Luton plant alone had four halls which were regularly used on Fridays and Saturdays (The Staff Canteen; Management Group Dining Room and the Red and Blue Rooms, Osborne Road) and for special occasions the Main Works Canteen.

Above 1963, and our first booking for a special modern (strict tempo) competition dance, held in the staff dining room at Vauxhall Motors, which were held regularly with young and old competing vigorously. A high degree of concentration and knowledge of tempos was required by the bands who played for them.

Left There were plenty of dinner dance dates for the town's bands, and, to meet the huge demand, some were put together just for one engagement, as this quartet probably was. So playing in the management group dining room at Vauxhall Motors (c. early 1970s) were: Les George (Double Bass); Keith Rolt (Piano); Brian Sapwell (Trumpet); Arthur Norman (Drums).

DANCE COMPETITIONS BRING HIGH STANDARD

THE HIGH standard of Ballroom and Latin American dancing made this year's Special Modern Dance in the Staff Dining Room in March, enjoyable for both participants and spectators.

The event attracted more than 250 people, with entries for the Senior and Junior competitions drawn from a wide area.

The results were:

Senior 4 Dance Open Amateur Competition for the Vauxhall Trophy:

1. Michael and Sheila Tailby (Kettering); 2. Michael and Doris Collins (Beckenham, Kent); 3. Peter Cavey and Pat Simons (Tolworth, Surrey); 4. David Douglas and Janice Barb (Southall and Boreham Wood).

Junior 4 Dance Open Latin American Competition for the Arthur Hutton Trophy:

1. Clive Taylor (Doncaster) and Jennifer Whiteley (Sheffield); 2. Stephen Crossley (Watford) and Carol Roberts (Slough); 3. Graham Large (High Wycombe)

Junior competition prizewinners, left to right, Carol Roberts, Stephen Crossley, Jennifer Whiteley and Clive Taylor, winners of the Arthur Hutton Trophy, Graham Large and Lynne Parsons

and Lynne Parsons (Feltham).

The cups and prizes were presented by Mr. and Mrs. Butt, Club Chairman and his wife.

The adjudicators, from London, were Ronnie Hutton, Bob More and Sydney Winter, with Mr. Arthur Hutton, Principal—Doe Howard School of Dancing, Barnet, as Scrutineer.

Competition stewards were: Messrs. W. Chamberlain, H. Allen, R. Butterfield and H. Baker.

The competitions were organised and compèred by Andy Anderson, Hon. Secretary of the Social Section, and dancing was to the music of the Barry Austyn Orchestra.

Senior Competition prizewinners and adjudicators are seen here with, left, Mr. and Mrs. Butt, and Andy Anderson. Janice Barb, Ronnie Hutton, Arthur Hutton, Bob More, Michael and Sheila Tailby, Michael and Doris Collins. Peter Cavey, Pat Simons, Sydney Winters (half hidden)

April, 1965
23

They were always held in high regard nationally, and the Vauxhall 'special modern dance' of March 1965 was reported in the April '65 edition of the Vauxhall Mirror, which shows the elegance of the dance competitors and the distance from whence they came to participate. The Barry Austyn Orchestra played for this one.

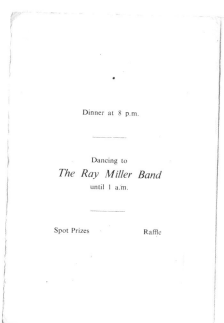

818 SOCIAL SECTION
VAUXHALL MOTORS LTD.
DUNSTABLE

present

A New Year Dinner & Dance

AT

THE BLUE ROOM
BRACHE ESTATE
LUTON

ON

Friday, 15th January, 1971

Dinner at 8 p.m.

Dancing to

The Ray Miller Band

until 1 a.m.

Spot Prizes   Raffle

Typical of the many weekly dinner dances held in the Vauxhall. This being a Dunstable social function held in the 'Blue Room' at The Brache, Luton.

Through going to the George Hotel Ballroom on a regular basis, I was getting to know all of the resident musicians as personal friends, and in particular Mark Fischer, whose sense of humour, generosity and advice made him a very warm and endearing character. He was genuinely interested in our 'young' band and volunteered to help at our rehearsals.

To have 'a big name' join the band, albeit for rehearsals, meant we had to have organised rehearsals, and a venue, because we had 'moved on' from the Specials Club, and Williamson Street was about to be pulled down as part of Luton's newly planned shopping precinct. Well, Mum and Dad suggested our house on Sunday mornings in Walcot Avenue!

The two downstairs rooms had been knocked into one, so 112 Walcot Avenue became the rehearsal room for the band. We had anything from 8 to 12 musicians blowing their heads off and, to their credit, the neighbours enjoyed it, and you could see

Late 1950s view of 112 Walcot Avenue – 'Rainbow House', the rehearsal rooms!

Brenda Bartini's trio at the Leicester Arms, Dunstable Rd, Luton 1957. Versatile Brenda, who also has accordion and clavioline keyboard on hand, wrote much of her own material. With Brenda are Jim Thompson (Drums) and Stuart Horn (Alto Sax).

windows open in Somerset Avenue and Walcot Avenue for easier listening. It wouldn't be accepted today. Mum always made tea and sandwiches, and then it was off to the Somerset Tavern for a few pints, with Mark of course, who was never allowed to buy a drink. During my research for this book, I was reminded by trumpeter John Scott that both he and John Murray (alto) came to Walcot Avenue as budding musicians, but for some reason things didn't work out. I didn't remember them, but it was certainly our loss.

We were starting to get work, albeit not weekly, which allowed us to rehearse like mad for the next engagement. Sometimes the booking would be for a quartet, but, so keen were we all to play, we would often turn up as a 6/7 piece. From the band's point of view this did us no harm, and enquiries for future bookings often resulted from our youthful and enthusiastic performances.

The presentation of our music was slick, because we always pre-picked the programme the night before each engagement, at Walcot Avenue, thus avoiding too much time wasting between each dance set. It was easy to pre-pick a dance programme, although very time consuming, as the dances then were always in sets. i.e. 3 Quicksteps, 2 Foxtrots, 2 Waltzes etc., etc.

The Men's Bar at the George was a regular focal point, but we entered 1959 still doing the village halls, clubs and working men's clubs, and some of the smaller Dinner Dance venues like the Leicester Arms, Biscot Mill and Somerset Tavern.

Mark Fischer lived in Grasmere Avenue, and his local was the Warden Tavern.

Occasionally we would pop up to the Warden to have a drink with him during the week. The landlord of the 'Warden' was Tommy Hodgson, the chairman/ manager of Luton Town F.C. and Luton had just reached the 1959 FA Cup Final! Unbeknown to us, Mark had been singing the praises of our band to Tommy, who out of the blue asked Mark if 'the lads would like to play at the Cresta Dance Hall for the Luton Town F.C. Cup Final Dance'. Would we? We were overwhelmed, and offered to waive the fee and play for Cup Final tickets! We knew it was our big chance – we needed to be at our best, and as the Dance would be on a Tuesday – 21st April '59, Mark could play with us! The town was on a high, and with the football team reaching Wembley, the atmosphere everywhere was electric. Being associated with the club at this time was unbelievable. The 3 members of the club, who were responsible for the dance, were Messrs. Ron Baynham, Syd Owen and Billy Bingham. Ron & Billy actually came to our house at Walcot Avenue to personally meet me and deliver 3 tickets as a "deposit"! Even though a fee wasn't requested, the club insisted on paying us £28-16s-0d (as well as the tickets) which the 3 players duly paid us after the dance. The Dance admission was 10s 6d. Ken, Mark and I went to Wembley together, and had a great day, although for the Town to lose 2–1 was a great disappointment.

Above We had no trouble augmenting the band at the 1959 Cup Final Dance, with the bonus of a final tie ticket available for everyone who played.

Right An internal view of the Cresta Ballroom, looking from the stage end to the bar. The original theatre balcony was left intact, for seating and viewing below.

The Ballroom is available for Private or Public Functions

Special Terms are available for Public Dances to Raise Funds

Details from the Manager without obligation

Luton Town Football and Athletic Co., Ltd.

'GRAMS
"FOOTBALL, LUTON"

SECRETARY
P. COLEY

REGISTERED OFFICE AND GROUND
70 - 72, KENILWORTH ROAD, LUTON

'PHONE: LUTON 3151

3rd April 1959.

S. Goodyear Esq
112. Walcot Avenue
Luton.

Dear Mr Goodyear, On behalf of the Luton Town Football Club, I wish to thank you for consenting to provide the music on the occasion of our Cup Final Dance to be held at the Cresta Ballroom on Tuesday 21st April 1959. My committee accept your quotation of £28-16-0, and look forward to a most enjoyable evening.

Yours very sincerely,
Syd Owen.

Luton Town F.C.
Kenilworth Rd.

Dear Stuart,

I am writing this letter on behalf of Syd Owen who I understand booked your band for our Cup Final Dance on 21st April. I would like to add my thanks for your services.

Now about the name I wonder could you come to the ground on Friday about 11.30 & we could discuss final arrangements as we all having a good high class cabaret. & their will be other things to sort out. I have enclosed 20 Complimentary tickets.

Yours Sincerely
Billy Bingham

Letters from Syd Owen (Luton Town F.C.'s Captain) booking our band for the Cup Final dance at the Cresta on Tuesday 21st April 1959, and from Billy Bingham (Luton winger) to finalise details of same function. Syd was capped by England and Billy played international football for Northern Ireland and later became their manager.

The Geoff Stokes Band, in carnival mood, at the Cresta, just before closure in 1960. Saxes, l. to r.: Geoff Stokes (with glasses), Charlie Goss, Dave Bradley, Eric Slaney (nearest camera). Brass, l. to r.: Ray Deakin (Trombone), Brain Sapwell (Trumpet), Jim Bull (Trumpet). Rhythm, l. to r.: Tom Stark (Piano), Jack Stone (Double Bass), Keith Burgoine (Drums). Conducting: Derek Tearle (Manager/M.C.).

By 1959/60 it was generally only local bands who were providing music for ballroom dancing at the Cresta, but ironically Tuesdays had become the most popular night, with the 'Jukes' playing the music of the day. Pete Green was the drummer/leader, with his brother Tony on guitar, Rory McGuinness (tenor sax); Ray Sills (piano); Dave Bavister (vocals – stage name Dave Baxter) and Vernon Critten (d/bass). The original pianist and leader of the Jukes was Colin 'Ray' Clarke who emigrated to Australia in 1957. The Cresta was demolished in July 1960.

On the 1st November 1961 I left the employ of D. Napier & Son and joined Vauxhall Motors Ltd.

Left (Three of) the Jukes at the Cresta Dome Ballroom (c.1959): Vernon 'Ted' Critten Jnr (Double Bass); Tony Green (Guitar/Vocals) and Peter Green (Drums), brothers.

The Norman Wesley Trio at the Halfway House. John Collier (Drums); Bert Humphreys (Alto Sax); Norman Wesley (Piano). They were probably supporting a larger band or group, as they are not centre stage.

Other venues were soon to open, which were to be as popular as their predecessors. The Majestic Ballroom, Mill Street, (the old Gaumont Cinema) – where the Roy Williams Orchestra was the most excellent resident band – and the California Ballroom (Dunstable) provided the very latest dance music and The Halfway House, Civic Hall (Dunstable), Hatters Club (Luton F.C.), Esso Motor Hotel and The Moat House (Moat Lane) were opened to meet the heavy demand for Dinner/Dance functions which reached their peak in the mid 1970s.

The Majestic Ballroom was one of the many dance halls that Top Rank (The Rank Organisation) opened throughout the country in the 1960s, and although the band was staffed with local semi-pro musicians, Rank had installed top pro Johnnie Woolaston from Preston as the leader, who was vigorous with his demands for musical excellence. I remember Roy Snape (trumpet), Tony Brinklow (tenor sax), Percy Jeffs (bass) and Freddie Wells (drums) as regular members. Roy Williams was in fact the stage name used by Roy Snape, but the hall was only open from about 1962–66.

The Old Gaumont Cinema, Mill Street, Luton, was soon to become a new dance hall.

The Roy Williams Orchestra was resident at the Majestic Ballroom, and featured Christine 'Tina' Lee & Bill Spence (Vocals) with Johnnie Woolaston (Leader/Conductor).

John Collier (Drums) and Norman Wesley (Piano) with their Quartet, fronted by Jackie Morrison (Sax) and Jack Snape (Trumpet), again at the Halfway House, Dunstable. In his formative years, Scotsman Jack joined an Irish Circus Band, which required him to learn another instrument, so he took up the cello. He also became lead trumpet in Nat Gonella's Band. In Luton, he gave trumpet lessons and taught John Scott, and played cello with a local Orchestra. His son Roy followed in his footsteps to become an excellent trumpeter.

Left The Old Moat House became a very popular venue for Dinner Dances and Wedding Receptions.

OPENING OF BEDFORDSHIRE'S LATEST MODERN BALLROOM
at the
HALFWAY HOUSE
DUNSTABLE

Mr. and Mrs. W. Creasey are pleased to announce the completion of the extensions to the hotel, which includes one of the finest ballrooms in the county. The appointments are luxurious, the special sprung maple floor will add to the pleasure of the dancers, and everything has been done for the comfort of our patrons.

OPENING NIGHT . . .
Saturday JANUARY 18
GRAND DINNER DANCE
7.30 p.m. to Midnight
LICENSED BARS • FINE FOOD
TICKETS **21/-** INCLUSIVE
DRESS OPTIONAL

SPECIAL GALA NIGHT
Saturday **FEBRUARY 1**
DINNER DANCE
With PERSONAL APPEARANCE of
BERNARD MONSHIN
AND
"RADIO'S ROMANTIC ORCHESTRA"

Dancing 7.30 to midnight   Evening Dress
LICENSED BARS • SPECIAL MENU
TICKETS **25/-** INCLUSIVE

Celebrate that special occasion by reserving a table NOW

HALFWAY HOUSE
DUNSTABLE • Phone Dunstable 80

Luncheons and dinners served daily
(except Sundays)

IT'S A WHITBREAD HOUSE

Right The opening of Bedfordshire's latest Modern Ballroom, at the Halfway House, Dunstable, on Saturday January 18th 1958. Destined to become the most popular of Dinner/Dance venues for years to come.

Below The pavilion at Hemel Hempstead was also an excellent concert and dance hall, and was a welcome addition to the area's venues when it opened in April 1966. Many Hemel firms held their functions there, as this programme and ticket, and I also saw the great American drummer Buddy Rich give a concert there with his Orchestra in the early 1970s.

Parker Fluidpower

ANNUAL DINNER DANCE
Friday, 12th January, 1979

at the
Culpin Room, Pavilion, Hemel Hempstead

Dinner 7.30 for 8.00 p.m.

Admission by Ticket only
£5.00   Dancing until 1.00 a.m.   Lounge suits
          LUCKY TICKET No. 93

Parker Fluidpower

ANNUAL DINNER DANCE

Friday, 12th January, 1979

at the
Culpin Room,
Pavilion,
Hemel Hempstead

Parker Fluidpower

LOYAL TOAST

Mr. G. C. Hoffman
Operations Manager — P & C Group, Hemel Hempstead

GUEST SPEAKER

Mr. R. C. Barnd
President, Parker Europe

Dancing to the Ray Miller Band

Flanked by Freddie Wells' Mum & Dad, the Johnny Kirkpatrick Trio playing in the
Connaught Rooms, 1952, for the 'American & Canadian War Brides Parents Association'!
Fred's eldest sister married a Canadian soldier. Freddie Wells (Drums); Les Hyde (Alto
Sax/Vocals and Harmonica); Johnny Kirkpatrick (Piano).

At 69, Freddie Wells, who was an evacuee to St. Albans at the outbreak of war,
still plays and teaches the drums with total dedication, and although he played at
the Majestic, he ran his own band, and was always on hand to help other bands if
available. I will always associate him as Jimmy Harrison's drummer, with whom he
has played since he was 21. Fred moved to Luton with his family when he was 18.

Jimmy Harrison (Keyboards) and Freddie Wells (Drums) unloading at the Halfway House,
Dunstable – 1960s.

The Top Rank Organisation also opened a 'Victor Silvester Studio' for Ballroom Dancing in the late 1960s at the Odeon cinema in Dunstable Road, which became a very popular social and dancing venue for beginners and exponents alike. Victor Silvester was famous for his ballroom orchestra which was regarded as the ultimate yard stick for strict tempo, and was used by the BBC for World Service Broadcasts. His reputation was synonymous with perfection, so it was commercially expedient for the Rank Organisation to endorse their studios with his name.

An evening's engagement was very tiring, some more than others. Friday evening bookings could be the most enjoyable of the weekend or the most arduous, because they were usually booked until 1.00am. Dinner functions that only required music for dancing were the best, and may have only necessitated an hour or two's music – after speeches. Whereas the Dinner functions that required music during the meal meant that the Rhythm section of the band (i.e. piano – myself, bass and drummer) would be on duty from (usually) 7.30 until 1.00am, with the rest of the band not required until about 10.00pm.

Some Friday bookings (which we only took when there was nothing else on offer) were just dances and, when booked from 8.00pm until 1.00am, were a real slog. If you turned up at 7.30pm and people were already sitting at their tables, with their 'patent' shoes and flasks of tea, you knew that by 1.00am the band would be totally exhausted. Most of these 5 hour dance functions tended to be in village halls, which didn't have the best of dance floors, and, to help the dancers 'glide', a chalk dust was sprinkled over the floor.

Saturday evenings were again either Dances or Dinner/Dances but always finished by midnight, and we would quite often fit in a Wedding Reception on a Saturday afternoon also!

To finish off the weekend we could guarantee a booking on Sunday evenings at any one of the many Social or Working Mens Clubs requiring our services after Bingo until 11.00pm.

Margaret, my wife, and the children never saw me on a Friday because I was in from

1975 – for Leighton Linslade Liberals.

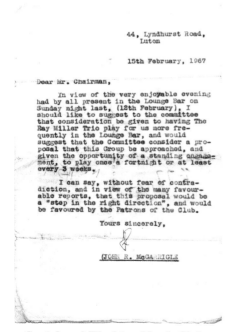

Social and Working Men's Clubs offered bands regular work throughout the year, so it was most gratifying to receive a copy of the above letter, from a member of Beech Hill Conservative Club.

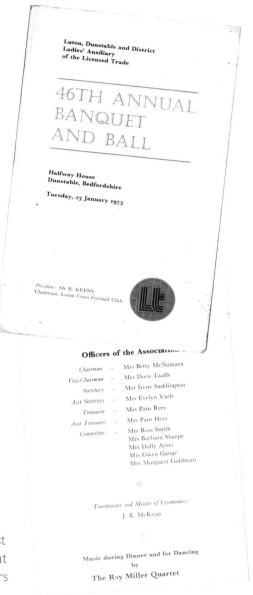

BIGGLESWADE ROUND TABLE
No. 497

Ladies' Night
Dinner-Dance

Friday, 15th March, 1968
THE BROADWAY HOTEL, LETCHWORTH

Chairman: H. R. CARLISLE, Esq.

Dancing to
RAY MILLER AND HIS
BAND

Master of Ceremonies:
NORMAN GILL, Esq.

Luton, Dunstable and District
Ladies' Auxiliary
of the Licensed Trade

46TH ANNUAL
BANQUET
AND BALL

Halfway House
Dunstable, Bedfordshire

Tuesday, 23 January 1973

President: Mr R. KEENS
Chairman, Luton Town Football Club

Officers of the Association

Chairman	–	Mrs Betty McNamara
Vice-Chairman	–	Mrs Doris Taaffe
Secretary	–	Mrs Irene Saddington
Asst Secretary	–	Mrs Evelyn Varle
Treasurer	–	Mrs Pam Rees
Asst Treasurer	–	Mrs Pam Heys
Committee:	–	Mrs Ross Smith
		Mrs Barbara Sharpe
		Mrs Dolly Ayres
		Mrs Gwen Gange
		Mrs Margaret Goldman

☆

Toastmaster and Master of Ceremonies:
J. B. McKean

☆

Music during Dinner and for Dancing
by
The Ray Miller Quartet

Above 1968 – at the Broadway Hotel, Letchworth.
Right There were also mid-week functions to fit in
as well – this one for the local landladies.

work and straight out by 6.00pm for most engagements. So, after a week's work at Vauxhall Motors, I would put in as many hours again at the weekends.

Associated with the dance halls was an etiquette that had been established with their formation. Apart from the odd couple, girls were always the first to make their entrance, from 8.00 p.m. – with not a man in sight until 9.30ish, at the earliest! Due to the absence of a male partner, most of the girls would have been dancing with each other up to the interval. After the interval, the lads would make their move and all the 'singles' would soon be partnered. To get the best lookers the 'gentlemen' had to be bold and quick off the mark, but it didn't always go to plan, as very often the 'lady' would refuse his request to dance, and he would return to his mates through a gauntlet of a hundred eyes, with dented pride.

That's how I met my Margaret, exactly as above, on a Thursday, at the Waterend Barn, St. Albans, and we have carried on dancing together for the rest of our lives.

Holding a complete stranger in your arms is difficult to imagine today, but that's how it was. The resident band at The Barn was Alex Miller.

Part of the fun at the dance halls was never knowing who you would meet – your wife perhaps? Meeting that someone special would eventually prove to be more difficult, with the demise of the public dance establishments. In the meantime every Saturday at 8.00 p.m. at every dance hall throughout the country, thousands of dancers would be 'tripping the light fantastic' with a Quick Step, the traditional start to every dance. Within 10 secs. most of them would have completed one circuit of the floor.

The following selection would give a typical hour's dancing, multiplied by 4 or 5 for a full evening's entertainment.

Come Dancing	}		Tea For Two Cha Cha Cha	}
Just One Of Those Things	} Quickstep		Petticoats Of Portugal (Tango)	} Latin
Zing Went The Strings Of My Heart	}		Mambo Jambo	} American
			Laughing Samba	}
Fascination	} Waltz			
Carolina Moon	}		Gay Gordons	}
			Dashing White Sergeant	} Old Tyme
Three Little Words	}		The Veleta	}
There's A Small Hotel	} Quickstep			
Jeepers Creepers	}		At The Hop	} Jive
			Jailhouse Rock	} Session
Just One More Chance	} Foxtrot		At The Jazz Band Ball	}
C'est Si Bon	}			
			Forever And Ever	} Old Tyme
			Que Sera Sera	} Waltz

Occasionally, the Bandleader or Master of Ceremonies would introduce a ladies/gentlemen's excuse me dance, meaning, you could tap a member of the opposite sex (i.e. someone you fancy) on the shoulder whilst they were dancing, for a dance. An invitation long since gone, I suspect!

As hard as it may be to realise today, it would be the norm for most youngsters who went dancing to dance sambas, tangos and most Latin American dances without hesitation. In fact, the musical director at the Bridge Hotel, Bedford was violinist Bernard Monshin, who fulfilled many exclusive engagements in the Home Counties with his Rio Tango Band, and regularly broadcast on the BBC Light Programme from the 1940s through the 50s.

Bandsmen often referred to the finale of an evening as a 'Cavalcade of Rubbish', when party numbers such as 'The Cokey Cokey'; 'The Conga'; 'Knees up Mother Brown', and 'Auld Lang Syne' etc. were traditional 'winding up' numbers.

The National Anthem was always played at the end of every function.

For many the evening wasn't finished there, as getting home was the next step, and for some it meant thumbing a lift home, although late buses were usually available. I vividly remember lines of girls outside 'The George' public house at Harpenden hitching lifts back to Luton, knowing they had a safety valve with the 12.20am Green Line bus if all else failed.

Geoff Stokes at the Cherry Tree, Welwyn Garden City, playing for a 'Christmas Do' (c. late 1950s). Lineup l. to. r.: Harold 'Schub' Stanton (Piano); Bob Smith (Guitar); Bob Stokes (Tenor Sax); Keith Burgoine (Drums); Cecil Capon (Alto Sax); Brian Sapwell (Trumpet); Geoff Stokes (Alto Sax); Jim Bull (Trumpet). Cecil Capon was the proprietor of the "Radio House" shop, Dunstable Road, opp. Luton & Dunstable Hospital.

Early Ray Miller Band December 1958 at the Winter Assembly Hall, Luton. Line-up: rhythm section: David Johns (Drums); Stuart Goodyear (Snr) (Double Bass); Yours truly (Piano); front row: Keith Indge (2nd Trumpet); Billy Lee (Lead trumpet); Brian Fielder (3rd Trumpet); Ken Hendley (2nd Alto Sax); Don Barrett (Lead Alto); Mark Fischer (Lead Tenor); Ken Tibbs (2nd Tenor Sax).

Another popular Hawaiian Orchestra of the 1940s was D'alberti.
Here l. to r. at the Leicester Arms: Heather Grainger (Vocals); Keith Dillingham (Guitar);
Bill Jones (Double Bass); Geoffrey D'alberti (Hawaiian Steel Guitar); Mel Colebrook
(Accordion); Derek Woodcroft (Guitar).

An early 1940s picture of pianist Spence Bell and his Band, with Charlie Goss (Alto Sax),
Eric Slaney, extreme right, (Tenor Sax) and Len Bolton (Trumpet). Others not known.

Memories of
Jazz, Skiffle and
Rock & Roll

by Peter Thompson

I joined Vauxhall Motors in the summer of 1955, as a student apprentice, and took eight years to complete the five year technical college course, for a number of very good reasons. These included girls and best bitter, but more especially my involvement with music.

My musical taste had already been flavoured by the New Orleans jazz revival bands which were beginning to appear on the best seller lists. I was in seventh heaven when I found that recording stars like Kenny Ball, Terry Lightfoot, Acker Bilk and Ken Collyer all appeared from time to time at the T.U.C. (Trade Union Club) jazz club in Church Street, Luton, always to packed houses. Collyer's line up included Chris Barber on trombone and a young fellow called Tony Donegan on banjo. During the interval he, Collyer and Barber (on bass) would stick around and, joined by Beryl Bryden on washboard, launch into intoxicating blues and folk songs. This was my introduction to what was to become Skiffle and to the man who was to evolve the genre almost single handed – Lonnie Donegan.

My arrival at Vauxhall coincided with preparations for the first ever apprentices' Rag Week; an excuse to cause total mayhem in the name of worthy causes. The driving force behind this event was the manic apprentice school instructor, Keith Riches, who never accepted "impossible" as a concept. He had a huge influence on us kids and was to remain a good friend for years. He was also a very good basketball player and he eventually kept the Fox pub, Dunstable Road, Luton, long since demolished in the name of progress. Keith was whipping up a frenzy of enthusiasm and none of us dared to tell him we could not think of a contribution to the big Saturday bash when George Street was to be descended upon.

A few of us decided to have a go at some of the Donegan/Collyer songs perched on the flat roof of the Corn Exchange public toilets on Market Hill. We knew most of the words by now and those we didn't could be covered by repeating other lyrics. The day dawned, and our motley crew took up position. It was a weird line up for any band. Arthur Childs on clarinet and Geoff King on banjo were the only two with any musical background and they were joined by Tony Robinson on washboard and myself on a contraption which passed as a double bass. I was standing atop an old oil drum thumping on a window sash cord tied to

In the late 1950s, you could see visiting top Dixieland Jazz Bands at either the Cresta Ballroom or the Trade Union Club, Church Street, on a regular weekly basis. This picture shows one of the most famous, Chris Barber, at the Cresta. His line up was: Chris Barber (Trombone) nearest camera; Pat Halcox (Trumpet); Monty Sunshine (Clarinet) farside; Jim Bray (Double Bass) facing camera. Others, not visible: Ron Bowden (Drums); Lonnie Donegan (Banjo).

a broom pole. Tony 'Robbo' Robinson had once played side drum in the cadet corps and was to become generally accepted as one of the great washboard players on the local Skiffle circuit. What we lacked in expertise we made up for in sheer enthusiasm and, as the day wore on, the initial handful of disbelieving shoppers was swelled by the arrival of growing numbers of teenagers who sensed a good day out was on the cards.

This was DIY music in its purest form and was instantly adopted by the kids. Live music until then had mostly been performed by dance bands and was associated with mum and dad's generation. To our astonishment every song was applauded and people were dancing. Having repeated our repertoire ad nauseam we eventually retired exhausted after being persuaded to do a couple of numbers at the rag dance that night. As far as I am aware this was the day the Luton Skiffle boom left the jazz clubs and reached a wider audience. It was also the day the Art Childs' jazzmen and the Pete Thompson Skiffle groups were born. Arthur was joined by Mick Cooper on trumpet and Bob Bates on trombone; Barry Collier played for both bands (on bass – later replaced by Pete Martin in Arthur's band), as did Geoff King and Robbo. John Leovold on guitar made up what soon became

The Pete Thompson Skiffle Group (c.1956). Line-up l. to r.: Geoff King (Banjo); Tony Robinson (Washboard); A.N.Other – wearing tie (guitar); Peter Thompson – at mic. (Vocals/Guitar); Julian Richardson (Drums).

a very solid Skiffle sound. Julian Richardson was a welcome, if occasional, addition to the Skiffle group on drums.

I took up banjo for a time but, since I had the loudest voice and did a passable impersonation of Lonnie Donegan, I was pressed into service as lead vocalist in both bands and the banjo is too noisy to sing over. Also, Geoff King was far and away the best banjoist around. I eventually learned guitar by studying Lonnie's educated left hand from the front row and practicing chord shapes from a dog eared roneo sheet that was passed around.

Luton was, at the time, a hotbed of live popular music. The glass-domed conservatory at the top of the Cresta Ballroom became the Delta jazz club one night a week. This was a showcase for local bands and was always packed to the rafters. One of the best local jazz bands was the Leaside Six who were probably the most polished Luton outfit and outlasted local competition by some time. A little after my day they became resident band at the Purple Turnip jazz club in Upper George Street (better known as the Connaught Rooms) above Arthur Day's music shop – admission 2 shillings (10p). They had, by then, become the Leaside Seven with the addition of a pianist. Our old compadre Bob Bates was their trombonist and he remembers the rest of the line-up as Harry Christian on clarinet, Trevor Evans on piano, Dick Kempson banjo, Noel Leat on drums, Philip (Pip) Hallman on double bass and John Goodwin on trumpet.

Four Members of the Leaside Six, complete with boaters, front a 'Girls High School Dance' group pictured at the Old St Mary's Hall, Church Street, Luton on April 5th 1958, with 250 dancers in attendance. Band members on parade l. to r.: Dick Kempson (Banjo); Trevor Evans (Piano); Harry Christian (Clarinet); Noel Leat (Drums); missing members Bob Bates (Trombone) and John Goodwin (Trumpet).

The Leaside Seven

Open

THE PURPLE TURNIP

Jazz Club

AT THE CONNAUGHT HALL
(Above Arthur Day's Music Shop)

FRIDAY 3rd APRIL 1959

Admission 2/-

7.30 – 11 p.m.

Left Handbill for 'The Purple Turnip' Jazz Club opening.

Right 'The Leasiders' Jazz Band, taken at 'The People' National Talent Contest, 1958. Line-up, back row l. to r.: Harry Christian (Clarinet); John Goodwin (Trumpet); Bob Bates (Trombone); front row, l. to r.: Dick Kempson (Banjo); Dave Nicholas (Washboard) note thimbles on fingers; Chris Plummer (Banjo).

The Leaside Six rehearsing above the Busy Bee Café, Bury Park 1958. Left to right: Harry Christian (Clarinet); John Goodwin (Trumpet); Trevor Evans (Piano); Bob Bates (Trombone); Dick Kempson (Banjo); Noel Leat (Drums).

Passing Lloyds Bank and Joe Lyons tea shop in George Street, the Leaside Seven in full swing on a float during a Luton College Rag Day Parade, late 1950s. Line-up: Philip 'Pip' Hallman (Sousaphone); Harry Christian (Clarinet); Chris Plummer (Banjo); John Goodwin (Trumpet); Bob Bates (Trombone); Dave Barton (Drums) and Trevor Evans on piano.

Johnnie Christmas and The Sunspots were unearthing songs that the rest of us had never heard and eventually developed their own distinctive style. The Vampires were working on a more professional version of the original Skiffle sound. George Woolhouse was ploughing his own furrow around the clubs and coffee bars as a very good solo blues and folk singer/guitarist (does anyone remember the Spider's Web in Guildford Street?). He would sit in occasionally with the band and even played with us once at Butlins but he preferred to perform alone.

As the Skiffle craze took off we found ourselves playing cabaret spots in local dance halls, pubs and coffee bars. I recall a couple of memorable Canal Boat Shuffles setting out from somewhere north of Leighton Buzzard. All the bands had their own followers who would turn up for every performance – heady days indeed.

Vauxhall, then, employed more than thirty thousand souls and had its own musical director. His name was Fred Green and, amongst other duties, he conducted the firm's orchestra and coached and conducted the Vauxhall girls' choir. This troupe was equal in quality to the more famous Luton girls' choir and, I'm pretty sure, sang on television on at least one occasion. Fred was another character who never took no for an answer. He used to organise a kind of road show from time to time and the Pete Thompson Skiffle group was added to the bill for a while.

The Vauxhall Male Voice Choir and the Vauxhall Ladies Choir combine to give a concert with the Vauxhall Orchestra in 1974, at the main Vauxhall works canteen.

Vauxhall Orchestra and Choir (c. mid 1960s). Ivor Pett (Euphonium), standing at the rear of Orchestra, also played with the Toddington Brass Band and played Saxophone in The Ray Miller Orchestra at the California Pool Ballroom, Dunstable during 1960.

HEL-LO VAUXHALL GIVE ME DOC-TOR JAZZ

GIVE ME DOCTOR JAZZ

To even the "squarest" by-stander it must be obvious that jazz is having a terrific boom in the district, and several Vauxhall musicians who make this form of relaxation a hobby have had a direct hand in producing this boom. Unfortunately, with this revived interest in jazz, there has also been a trend towards rock'n'roll which proves the theory that much of the Luton youth is "jazzy" minded rather than jazz minded. This trend, however, has been ignored by the musician and by the true jazz enthusiast.

As the styles of jazz vary, so do the musicians, and within Vauxhall we have a fair sprinkling of "trad-men," "bop-boys" and "skifflers" each of whom plays mainly for the love of his own particular style, as our investigation on this page will prove.

While the musicians argue amongst themselves regarding the merits of their various favourites, and their fans about the quality of their music then jazz will remain healthy and thriving in Luton in general and Vauxhall in particular.

favourite kind of jazz has a late 20's early 30's flavour.

"Good jazz, like beauty, is impossible to define and is therefore a matter of individual perception. It is best played in a small room, for love of it rather than for money."

Freddie Wells (Cost Office)—Drums

We found Freddie very broad-minded in his attitude towards

Georgie "Mose" Woolhouse (Laboratory)—Guitar and Vocal

Applauding audiences have no attraction for Georgie for his only real musical interest is blues singing. He started off by playing a mouth organ, later taking up the four-string guitar both of which he has played in local jazz clubs and cafes for some time.

"Apart from blues I appreciate New Orleans jazz. Luton's jazz fans? They make me sick. In my estimation 95 per cent. of them are mere rock'n'rollers. Modern jazz? A fascinating idiom—for those playing it."

Pete Thompson (Apprentice A.C. Inspection)—Guitar and Vocal

Unlike Georgie Woolhouse, Pete plays to the crowds and has done much to popularise skiffle in Luton. His group is mostly a section of the original Art Childs' Jazzmen, incorporating Geoff King and Tony Robinson.

Of skiffle groups in general he said:

"Most groups are formed by young lads who can't afford instruments and who want to make music. Fair enough, it's all good fun, but so many of them don't realise that skiffle is good American (mostly Negro) folk music and has a meaning to it. Rock'n'roll? All rock'n'roll numbers are composed around five tunes at the most—nothing whatsoever remotely to do with skiffle."

8

Tony "Robo" Robinson (Apprentice Jig Shop) —Washboard

Generally considered the local best on washboard, "Robo" provides much of the driving, bouncy rhythm prevalent in the Pete Thompson Skiffle Group, and by watching and hearing him play, those who scorn will realise that not anyone can pick up a washboard and play it. He has modestly brushed aside many suggestions that with a little practice he could become a great boogie pianist. He is at present saving up to buy an electric washing machine. He says: "I am strictly a New Orleans fan but I can also appreciate classical music. I deplore rock'n'roll."

George Coleman (Pattern Shop)—Piano

George, although better known as an Olympic walker, is appreciated by many as a modern style jazz pianist. He is seen on next page playing a duet with E. MacDonald Bailey, the famous sprinter.

When asked for a comment on the subject, George said: "Jazz? I find all kinds interesting but not necessarily satisfying. My opinions are that so-called modern jazz is too cold and calculated, skiffle a bit rough and ready, rock'n'roll should be seen and not heard, and that traditional jazz is not bad but it is inclined to dogmatism. My

Picture above: Pete Thompson, who sings and plays the guitar with Jim Collins, trombonist

Rex Woodley slaps that double bass

Centre spread of Thursday August 22nd 1957 issue of Vauxhall Mirror. "Give me Doctor Jazz".

jazz masters. His main love lies in " mainstream " jazz, which is, for those who are rather lost on the subject, roughly a type of music which incorporates the styles of both " trad " and modern. When approached he had the following to say: " Jazz has a short history and a long tradition. Let's forget tradition, shelve the history, and concentrate on the advancement of music."

Art Childs (Chaul End) —Clarinet

Art Childs (of whom Art Childs once said, " Improves with every outing ") is another classical music lover. He formed a group to play in various doorways during the 1956 Apprentices Rag and has since gone from

music as his recent interests show. He is at present drumming with the Jimmy Harrison Band, the Davis Orchestra and the Vauxhall Motors Orchestra.

He says, " jazz is a musician's individual improvisation on a melody, in most cases a well-known one. To play it you must be in the mood and it must come from the heart. My interest is inclined towards modern jazz although I admit that " trad " is the foundation stone of all modern jazz. Duke Ellington, Stan Kenton and Tony Kinsey are among my favourite bands and as regards drumming I am greatly influenced by the styles of Eric Delaney, Jack Collier and Ray Price."

Rex Woodley (Cost Office)—Bass

An unassuming young man, Rex was schooled with the Congreve Youth Orchestra and remained " long-hair " until he was persuaded to have a " go " at an Apprentice Jam Session. He has played skiffle for laughs but is at heart a modernist. He has definite opinions about the various jazz styles.

" I prefer playing modern jazz because a musician is required rather than an exhibitionist. Traditional jazz is merely a repetition of corny chords and hackneyed phrases supported by

a miserable imitation of a rhythm section. Although jazz is essentially improvisation I like to play Count Basie and Duke Ellington arrangements.

" Skiffle ? O.K. for non-musicians.

" Rock'n'roll ? Trash."

Jim Collins (Service) —Trombone

Jim has become popular locally as a " trad " trombonist with the Wayfarers Jazz Band, but deplores the worshipping of old

strength to strength. He now leads one of the leading local " trad " bands but appreciates many types of music.

" I am equally as fond of classic music as I am of ' trad,' in fact I still play a lot of classical. I also appreciate good modern jazz when played by good musicians, for example, Gerry Mulligan."

Geoff King (Electrical Apprentice)—Banjo

In local jazz circles Geoff is held in high esteem. He is a technician and appreciates all good original New Orleans jazz. He insists on remaining in the background with both the Art Childs' Jazzmen and the Pete Thompson Skiffle Unit, for whom he plays, but seems to drive to the fore with his considerable technique. His comments referred mainly to his own particular instrument:

" Traditional jazz and skiffle are helping a great deal to bring back the popularity of the banjo, which has not, for some years, been considered a serious instrument. At present it is still only a background instrument but I am sure that it will again become as popular as the guitar."

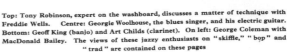

Top: Tony Robinson, expert on the washboard, discusses a matter of technique with Freddie Wells. Centre: Georgie Woolhouse, the blues singer, and his electric guitar. Bottom: Geoff King (banjo) and Art Childs (clarinet). On left: George Coleman with MacDonald Bailey. The views of these jazzy enthusiasts on "skiffle," "bop" and "trad" are contained on these pages

LUTON INDUSTRIAL MISSION AND COMMUNITY CENTRE

Headquarters:
Chapel Street Methodist Church, Luton

GRAND

VARIETY CONCERT

Thursday, 14th March 1957

At 7.15 p.m.

— WITH —

- **VAUXHALL MOTORS GIRLS' CHOIR** •
- **THE MUDLARKS** • **HAROLD MOON**
- **MARIE JEFFS AND DAVE CUNNINGHAM** •
- **RITA CHRISTIAN** •
- **CHRISTINE AND ROSEMARIE** •
- **ART CHILDS AND HIS JAZZMEN** •
- **PETER THOMPSON AND HIS SKIFFLE GROUP** •
- **ROY SHACKLETON** •

ADMISSION BY PROGRAMME - - ONE SHILLING

PROCEEDS FOR INDUSTRIAL MISSION

JOHN T MERRY, PRINTERS, LUTON

A poster for one of Fred Green's variety concerts, organised for, and held at, the Luton Industrial Mission, and what a line up! The Mudlarks were destined to be top international recording stars, with a string of records in the hit parade. In March 1959 Geoff Mudd was conscripted into the Army, and David Lane became the new member to join Mary & Freddie. Peter Thompson is coincidentally on the same bill as his wife-to-be Rosemarie, and future father-in-law, Harold Moon.

The majority of the multitude of employees was fed daily in the cavernous main canteen on a three shift system. Fred's concert party, including us, played three consecutive concerts in three hours, each time to an audience that would have filled the Albert Hall. We were once bussed down to the Walthamstow pavilion for a show (why there I never found out) and I still have a poster of another concert we all did at the Mission Centre Hall in Chapel Street.

It was all becoming a bit hectic. We were all students whose priority should have been qualifying for our chosen trade and there was no chance of making any real money. We could afford a few more beers than our non-musical contemporaries but that was about it.

This was true of Skiffle generally. Our experience was being repeated in every town in the country but only Lonnie

Performing at the concert was magician Harold Moon of Cutenhoe Road, and his assistant – daughter Rosemarie. Rosemarie and Christine were on the bill in their own right as a tap dancing duo. Live backing music would have been on hand to support each act as necessary.

was to make a big time career out of it. Chas McDevitt, Nancy Whisky, The Vipers and Johnny Duncan were well know and made a few records but the survivors had to change their styles to stay in work.

For whatever reasons my own group decided to call it a day and some of them moved on to other ventures. Robbo joined The Sunspots and performed on a couple of tracks recorded after a Skiffle contest. The album, including several other bands, is still available to this day. At that time he was playing harmonica and very rarely returned to the washboard. I had been approached earlier by Dick Carlton, the leader of The Vampires, with a view to combining the talents of both bands but, at the time, we probably had the best following locally and I saw no reason to change. Now seemed a good time to give it a go so, resplendent in my outfit – all black with a gold vampire on the shirt – I lined up as lead singer and rhythm guitarist with The Vampires.

Skiffle contests were all the thing then. It was a way for record companies to sift through the plethora of groups banging away all over the country, in the hope of finding a gold nugget hidden in some obscure location. Every contest claimed to be the definitive U.K. national knockout and the prize was the opportunity to have a record released. We, of course, signed up and battled our way through heats and the quarter finals at the Streatham Locarno to be invited, exhausted but triumphant, to the Cafe de Paris in the West End for the semi finals.

Titbits Magazine did a feature on "Luton's Vampires" and we thought we were a bit special. The line-up was myself, Dick Carlton and Alan Johnson on guitars, Harry Gillis on washboard, Pete Cameron on bass and Nifty Niven on drums. Nifty, in addition to an ambition to become Luton's Gene Krupa, had one priceless asset. He worked for the electricity board and got to bring the van home at weekends, which we were able to use! Dave Waller completed the group on banjo. It was a good sound in its day and, with some nice harmony in our locker, we were moving on from pure Skiffle.

We were told, unofficially, that we had made the final along with three other bands, but the weeks went by and the organisers remained spectacularly silent. The truth eventually dawned on us that the Skiffle boom was ever so slightly on the wane and the money available for studio time and promotion was being diverted to other styles, many of which had been spawned by the raw, high energy Skiffle sound. In the end the final was never contested.

At the time I was in digs and shared the top room in the turret on the corner of West Hill Road and London Road with the landlady's son, Colin Field. He was a good mate of mine and, boy, could he dance. Unfortunately, he had a habit of indulging in his two favourite pastimes at the same time, sometimes until the small hours. These were practising the drums clad only in his jocks, with a sun ray lamp on full beam mounted on a stand behind him. Sleep was elusive.

Evolution is inevitable and Skiffle would not escape it. In the beginning the movement was anchored to the New Orleans revival bands ("Trad" as the sound was called) but very soon it was latched on to by kids who were bursting to make music, who had no jazz background whatsoever and who thought nothing of throwing in the occasional Rock 'n' Roll number. When I joined The Vampires I was the only jazzman in the group, whereas our original band had been made up entirely of jazzmen.

Today it is perfectly acceptable to enjoy music of any denomination, but in the fifties alliance to a specific genre was expected and would even determine your social group to some extent. Trad / Skiffle types never confessed to liking a modern jazz piece and followers of neither style ever risked being accused of listening to Rock and Roll.

In a way Skiffle had forsaken its roots. There was also the problem of the limited repertoire slavishly copied from the handful of recording bands with no attempt by most groups to develop their own character. It was very basic music; none of us ever claimed it required highly proficient instrumentalists and the real musicians, perhaps with some justification, looked down their noses at it. But no one could

IT'S SKIFFLE and ROCK 'n' ROLL for LUTON'S VAMPIRES

By MARGARET McCARTNEY

ONE of the joys of being a skiffler is that you don't know where it is going to lead you. From making the grade with the local over-sixties club, you may find yourself suddenly whisked away to the plush luxury of London's Café de Paris.

And that's really what happened to the Vampires, one of the brightest of the modern do-it-yourself music making groups in Luton, which as everyone knows is also famous for boaters and motors and the Luton Girls' Choir.

In spite of playing on those sacred steps down which Noel Coward, Sophie Tucker and that glamorous grandmother Dietrich have trod (in exchange for a few thousand pounds), the Luton Vampires have retained their sense of proportion. Their moment of glory was in answer, not to a diamond-studded contract, but a Skiffle Contest.

Making up the Vampire group are: Peter Thompson, Alan Johnson and Dick Carleton, guitars; Pete Cameron, tea chest; Harry Ghillies, washboard, and "Nifty" Niven, drums.

Peter, Alan, Pete and Harry are all General Motors boys while "Nifty" is an electrician an Dick an engineer.

When they are not building cars, or helping to make the wheels of Luton's industry go round, they are beating out their numbers of the washboard, rolling out the rhythm on the drums.

If they have a group gimmick, it is a negative one. No beards! For them the 'skiffle scrub' is definitely out. They are strictly in favour of the close shave—to a man.

But they go for side-boards, as well as washboards, and all six of these skifflers have a slightly understated Edwardian air. Sober-clad in their black shirts and pants, they would have their fans believe that black hearts beat—to the rhythm of the navy blues of course—beneath the yellow badges on their breasts.

If you ask them why they call themselves the Vampires, they will side step neatly by denying that it is because they are blood suckers.

"No, sir," says Peter, "We don't play for profit." But they do admit that one of their firm favourites is "Greenback Dollar."

Which seems to prove they are strictly traditionalists.

They like to get together and arrange their own versions of these folksongs they play—occasionally even rewriting the words.

With a signature tune like "Streamline Train," they certainly have what it takes to go places.

Their list of dates is long and varied. It ranges from Luton's Cresta Ballroom, to concerts and dances at Walthamstow Pavilion and local 'hops'.

And wherever the Vampires are playing they have a following of fans, of all ages and both sexes.

Unlike so many of the skiffle groups, they don't mind a bit of honest-to-goodness "Rock 'n' Roll."

"'Rocking around the clock' is one way of expressing ourselves, 'Worried man blues' is another. The skiffle world is big enough for both." So says Peter, whose tastes are commendably catholic.

His interests are varied too—like most of the group, he finds plenty of time for girl friends.

They are not, so to speak, wedded to their washboards, dedicated to their drums.

Only Pete is a strictly bachelor type. With him it's rugger and not romance that rivals skiffle in his heart.

The Vampires have overcome the practising problem in a unique way. They practice before their audiences! And what's more, their audiences haven't yet caught up with the fact. Which seems to prove the point somewhere!

Perhaps the point is that the group has really got together and works as a team, anticipating each others' reactions, knowing just how one and another will take a certain phrase, interpret a certain score. And that, say the Vampires, is the secret of their success. They are a six-man group whose heart, and rhythm beats are one.

THE VAMPIRES

"Its Skiffle and Rock 'n' Roll for Luton's Vampires" – at the Cresta Ballroom.

deny its popularity and the excitement it brought to the era.

So, after maybe three years, the music in its popular form had run its course. Many of the original Skiffle haunts embraced the growing interest in "folk music" which allowed a much broader span of styles to be presented. The resulting movement survives and can be found in the Luton area to this day. Also, the jazz bands that Skiffle sprang from still have a devoted following. Chris Barber tours regularly with many of the old names on board. Lonnie, way out the most charismatic and talented singer and musician of his time, pops up from time to time as good as he ever was. Bob Bates and his band can be heard regularly at local events around Luton and Bob gets better every time I hear him, although he tends to play sousaphone more than trombone nowadays.

Only eighteen months or so ago I was fortunate enough to be at the Royal Albert Hall for a grand Skiffle re-union. The place was packed and the stars who admitted to owing their first break to Skiffle were too numerous to list. Many of them did a couple of numbers in the first half and left the whole of the second half to Lonnie. A portly (aren't many of us by now?) Chas. McDevitt strode on stage at the start and shouted "anybody here who played in a Skiffle group?" A roar of "yes" came in unison from thousands of throats and as many hands shot into the night air. Fraternity was instant, the atmosphere was magical and the massed choir belted out the well remembered words from forty odd years ago for four hours.

The original Deep South blues and folk songs from the beginning of the twentieth century are still played and are the basis of all jazz and rock. A massive spread of popular music has fanned out from those beginnings, with some help from hillbilly and country styles, and continues so to do. The Rolling Stones, for instance, have trawled the same musical waters for inspiration as the Skifflers did years before, to much greater effect it has to be said. Many famous super stars cut their performing teeth in unknown Skiffle bands of the fifties. These include Mick Jagger, The Beatles, The Shadows, Cliff Richard – the list is endless.

On a historical note the word "Skiffle" originates from the twenties in New Orleans. If you couldn't pay the rent and eviction loomed you threw a "Skiffle". It was open house and everyone in the neighbourhood showed up with booze and musical instruments, many of them home made. On their way out folk would chip in what they could and disaster was averted. Those must have been some parties!

The earliest use of the word in the U.K. I have been able to trace is 1951/2 when the Humphrey Lyttelton band was augmented by a small group of blues enthusiasts. Humph, aware of the original meaning and musical influence, called these sessions "Skiffles" but, as far as I know, it wasn't used to describe the music until the Collyer / Barber / Donegan era of the mid fifties. It is noteworthy that Beryl Bryden, the late blues singer, was playing washboard with a blues band around the clubs as long ago as the late forties.

Anyway, to return to Luton and to continue.

In the mid to late fifties Luton was host to some of the world's greatest swing bands. The Cresta Ballroom in Manchester Street (the Alma Theatre in an earlier life) would be converted into a concert hall overnight. In spite of my "trad"

The Duke of Bedford on a Tea-chest Bass, skiffles along with Chris Morris on guitar and Trevor Evans on washboard. At the time (c.1958) the Duke embarked on a series of PR visits in the area, and is shown here at the Leagrave Drill Hall. Trevor would have been happier with a piano!

beginnings I saw and heard, among others, live appearances by Ted Heath, Lionel Hampton, Duke Ellington, Tubby Hayes and Stan Kenton. In those days Londoners would travel to Luton to catch the greats.

The resident band at the Cresta then was the Don Smith orchestra. The Pete Thompson Skiffle group occasionally did the interval spot while Don's boys nipped out for a pint. On one such evening the Duke of Bedford made a surprise entry to publicise the Woburn Tours. His agent had convinced him that it would be a good stunt to sit in with a Skiffle group to attract a younger clientele. Why does everybody who's never done it assume that playing the washboard is a piece of cake? In the Duke's case there was a total absence of natural talent. He wrecked our show to the point where people were leaving and then he vanished into the night. Somewhere in the vaults at the Luton News I'll bet the photo still exists.

Did someone mention Rock & Roll?

The world had not come to terms with the burgeoning Rock & Roll revolution at that time. Whilst still at school the only chance we had to hear the latest music was with one ear glued to the wireless trying to listen through the interference to Radio Luxemburg. We had been fed on a diet of swing and Dickie Valentine ballads for years until one night in December 1954 Bill Haley came into our lives, "One two three o' clock ——-" the world would never be the same again. In a short time many names were to become legends singing and playing the music that, in spite of consistent attempts by authority to put it down, would influence the world of popular song more than any other.

In May 1956 came another monumental event. I was on a high stool in Steve's cafe in Park Street next door to the Salvation Army Temple, stirring my tea with the only spoon in the establishment, which was attached firmly to the counter by a length of lavatory chain. Tea with a Lyons fruit pie was standard fare while you were waiting to start the evening session at college. Someone put a tanner in the jukebox and Elvis hit us for the first time with Blue Suede Shoes—the hell with authority, we were hooked.

Back to the Cresta. The only opportunity we had to listen to live Rock & Roll in those days was from whichever dance band was playing in the local hall. They would play the standard programme all night during which jiving was banned. This was to allow the "Come Dancing" brigade to flit around the perimeter of the floor without colliding with a gyrating Ted. To make this period of the evening bearable the Teddy Boys invented "The Creep". This roughly involved moving each crepe sole a maximum of two inches with your groin locked to your partner's. The bloke's right hand rested on the girl's rump and the left held her right with arms at full stretch towards the floor. The patron saint of "The Creep" was Ted Heath who wrote the original song and whose "Hot Toddy" also had the perfect rhythm for the dance. For the three numbers before the last waltz, however, the band would play heavily sanitized versions of the current Rock and Roll hits. The Ballroom dancing lot would sniff and start looking for their cloakroom tickets while the dance floor became an animated, colourful mass of humanity. Jive to us was the epitome of pure cool – none of the American stuff you saw at the pictures with girls flying between your legs and such. The girl was spun clockwise through 360 degrees then immediately back again. You never, ever sent the girl anti-clockwise first. The bloke directed and controlled this activity solely with his right hand and a standard foot action that involved the minimum of movement. He would very occasionally return the girl with his left hand but only perhaps three or four times in an evening. Also, he would sometimes perform his own brand of fancy footwork but this was brief and rare. His left arm always hung loose at his side – cool.

When the Teddy Boy fashion was superseded by the Italian "Bumfreezer" box jacket the jive was refined further. The accompanying winkle picker, smooth soled shoes permitted the guys much more movement and fancier footwork. The girl was perpetually spinning, ballerina like, and the top of her head never changed height. The fella, on the other hand, would bob in perfect sequence with every other man in the hall, something to do with the steps, I assumed. I played many times on stage in front of such a crowd and from my elevated position I used to marvel at this synchronised action.

This scenario was to be observed at all the local dance halls; the Cresta, The George Hotel ballroom on a Thursday night, the public hall at Harpenden on Saturdays to the strains of the Geoff Stokes orchestra. My cousin, Stuart Goodyear, was leader of the very popular Ray Miller orchestra but he is already filling you up on that story. The George Hotel, incidentally, was on George Street, pre-Arndale somewhere adjacent to Littlewoods front entrance today, and was an essential venue on the weekly round of places to be seen.

SAMUEL WHITBREAD 1720-1796

LUTON AND DISTRICT
LICENSED VICTUALLERS' PROTECTION ASSOCIATION
(Est. 1874)

CENTENARY
BANQUET AND BALL
QUEENSWAY HALL, DUNSTABLE
13th MARCH, 1974

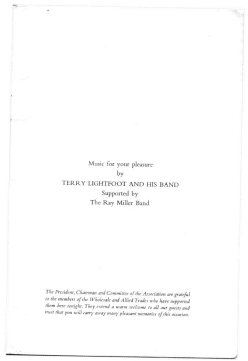

Music for your pleasure
by
TERRY LIGHTFOOT AND HIS BAND
Supported by
The Ray Miller Band

The President, Chairman and Committee of the Association are grateful
to the members of the Wholesale and Allied Trades who have supported
them here tonight. They extend a warm welcome to all our guests and
trust that you will carry away many pleasant memories of this occasion.

Ray Miller sharing the evening with top recording Jazz band Terry Lightfoot, at the Queensway Hall, Dunstable.

It should be mentioned here that a very different style of jiving had been developed in the jazz clubs. The man was more active and probably rotated as much as the girl. His footwork involved much stomping in a curious motion with knees locked half bent. Free hands and arms would flail in a wide radius and there was a definite hesitation when connected hands reached the top of the turn.

Once you had mastered either of these styles it was impossible to switch to the other. Your chosen culture seemed to be ingrained in the limbs.

The Rock & Roll and Skiffle booms were born and progressed at pretty much the same time, so to be involved with both was almost a full time occupation. Hence my need to take eight years to complete a five-year engineering course.

I learned, only a few months ago, that Elvis's early TV spectaculars featured some of the same songs that the Skifflers were performing at the same time. He was accompanied by famous orchestras and gospel choirs of course, while we had washboards and tea chests. On reflection our sound was far more authentic.

Luton's most famous vocal group by far in those days was the Mudlarks. They, also, were employed by Vauxhall Motors and were members of the Fred Green concert party. Mary, Freddie and Geoff were the nicest people you ever met and never allowed their fame to interfere with their roots and their friendships. They played the same halls as us for months but with much more class. It was obvious from the first time we heard them that they were going places. Our Skiffle group played the warm up spot for the Mudlarks on several occasions and we got to know them quite well. When Geoff finished his apprenticeship he was immediately called up for the army. I was vaguely approached as to whether I would be able to stand in but, by now, they were appearing regularly on TV – Six Five Special and various variety shows. "Lollipop" had gone to number two in the top twenty and "Book of Love" was on its way to number eight. Sensibly, there was no way I could have got involved and still been able to complete my training. Also, the music business had already proved itself to be mighty precarious, even if you had real talent and something very special to offer, so the decision would not have been a difficult one. I admit, however, to being very flattered and, to be honest, scared to death.

If I had needed any guidance with this decision, which I didn't, enter my dad. He was a tough little Geordie who had spent most of his working life from his fourteenth birthday down a coal mine. During the war years he had been a riveter in an aircraft factory until he eventually found a less demanding haven at Vauxhall. The greatest gifts he could bestow upon his son were indentures and a skilled trade. To this end he had uprooted home and family to give me a better start. He was not about to stand idly by while I, as he put it, "ran away to the circus".

Another great Luton band at that time was Mike Dean and The Kinsmen who played mainly at The George Ballroom. I have no idea if they ever made a living out of it in the end but they should have. It is possible that they were so expert at reproducing the hit sounds of the day that they didn't find their own style. I heard very recently that they played the warm up for The Beatles at the Majestic Ballroom, Luton, in the early sixties. How about having that on your CV?

After my time, I'm afraid.

As Skiffle faded I moved over to Rock & Roll and set up another band from the remnants of The Vampires and our original group. The front line included Alan Johnson and myself, with Arthur Childs playing Rock & Roll saxophone solos on clarinet – unique I think in those days. Our repertoire involved mainly Everly Brothers and Buddy Holly hits and we were playing, more or less, the same venues as the old Skiffle group had, post jazz club days.

As the decade approached its end marriage loomed and the need to earn a living stared me in the face. Maturity has eluded me to this day, but the onset of responsibility restrained the wilder instincts. So, we all went our separate ways to various levels of respectability.

I would not take a million quid for my teenage years. Those who followed us in the sixties would have you believe that they dragged music out of the dark ages. Absolute nonsense – my generation invented Rock & Roll!!! The excitement and sheer buzz in Luton in the mid to late fifties was palpable. This might have been true everywhere else, but Luton was where I happened to be at the time.

Will Skiffle in its original form ever make a big comeback? Well, I have a grandson, just over a year old, who is called Lonnie – really – not a nickname!, who knows?.

P.S. (Lonnie Donegan: b.Anthony James Donegan, d.November 3rd 2002)

Pete Thompson and his Rock & Roll group (c.1958). Personnel l. to r.: Alan Johnson; A.N.Other (Guitar/Vocals); Arthur Childs (Clarinet); Peter Thompson (Guitar/Vocals). Arthur Childs also ran his own jazz band.

Chris Morris was another young group emerging in the 1950s to play in the Rock & Roll idiom. L. to r.: Dick Kempson (Banjo); Chris Morris (Drums); Vernon 'Ted' Critten (Jnr) (Bass); Unknown (Guitar).

The Ray Miller Orchestra

Augmenting up to a 12, 13, or 14 piece orchestra from a 6/7 piece band seemed to happen overnight and, having done it, we were about to enter a tremendously exciting period from 1959 over the next 3 to 4 years. The success of the Cup Final dance, together with the many plaudits our orchestra received, made us determined to keep the outfit together at that size. It did mean stepping up a gear to get 'better work', but David and I set to the task

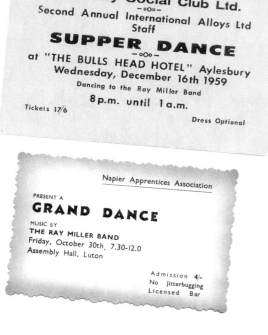

1959, and beginning to consolidate our contacts, with a look at tickets and poster from random engagements.

The California Pool Ballroom, Dunstable. Not the prettiest of buildings, but nonetheless very popular and successful – and a good friend to us.

with youthful exuberance and, it has to be said, we had a fair amount of success. We were to be known as 'The Luton Band With London Reputation', and used this on our notepaper. News was out that a new big dance venue was being built at the foot of the Dunstable Downs, which was to be known as the California Ballroom. Eddie Green was the owner of the hall being built at Dunstable, and I cannot remember how contact was made with him, but it resulted in us being invited to rehearse at the hall whilst it was being built, with the intention of becoming the resident band when it opened. We were making excellent progress, attracting a strong nucleus of about 12 musicians as permanent band members. We were to share the residency with Russ Sainty and Rhet Stoller with the Nu-Notes, and the opening night set the pattern for many a Saturday to come.

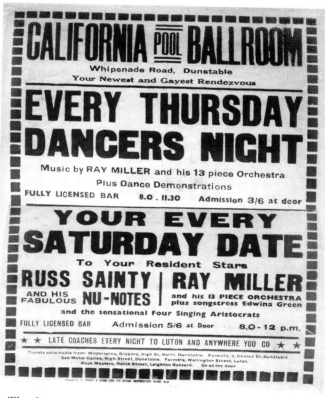

The first poster to publicise the weekly programme at the 'Cali' during 1960.

The Ray Miller Orchestra, March 1960, at the California Pool Ballroom, Dunstable. Line-up: Rhythm section: Jack Dove (Piano); Stuart Goodyear (Snr) (Double Bass); David Johns (Drums); Saxophones l. to r.: Ivor Pett (Baritone); Frank Pipkin (2nd Alto); Don Barrett (Lead Alto); Tom Lloyd (Lead Tenor); Ken Tibbs (2nd Tenor); Brass l. to r.: Eric Linney (3rd Trumpet); Billy Lee (Lead Trumpet); Keith Indge (2nd Trumpet); Don Excell (Trombone); Conductor/M.C.: Stuart Goodyear (Jnr) (Standing).

Eddie Green appointed Alex Brightman as hall manager to run the entertainment, which proved to be a wise move. His knowledge and association with professional entertainment was to be of immense benefit to us, as well as the overall presentation and organisation of the hall's events.

We had the orchestrations, and our wardrobe was smart with contrasting light blue jackets/silver grey lapels and black evening trousers. We had 3–4 spare jackets made, ranging from medium to extra large, which was going to prove to be a prudent decision.

Alex Brightman also made the suggestion that the band would be better presented if I fronted it, as M.C./vocalist etc., to add a touch of personality. I froze at the thought, but gradually eased myself into it and, it has to be said, the experience laid the foundations for the next 25 years with me leading the band. It meant bringing in a pianist, and Cecil Arnold and Norman Thompson were the two locals who shared this mantle, when we put out a band that I fronted. I still played piano when we went out on a smaller function. The very first number I ever sang was "Itsy Witsy Teeny Weeny Yellow Polka Dot Bikini", which as a Cha Cha, was all the rage!

Unbeknown to us at the time, Eddie Green's daughter Edwina was a talented singer, and it was mutually agreed that Edwina would be an asset to the band, with a view to the California residency, if she slotted in. Although she was only about 17, Edwina came out with the band at many of our engagements prior to the Cali

Resident with the Ray Miller Orchestra at the California Ballroom was Russ Sainty and his Nu-Notes, featuring Rhett Stoller on lead guitar (both shown here).

opening, and also sang with us at rehearsals. She did well, and became part and parcel of the band. I remember her knockout number as being 'Someday' (You'll want me to want you)! Through her youngest brother Christopher, I have been able to make contact with Edwina and found her as Mrs. Hillier, running a Guest House in Burchetts Green, Nr. Maidenhead. She had unfortunately lost her husband.

Rehearsing at the Cali was usually on a Sunday morning, and at first the hall was nowhere near completion, so we were often playing and watching plasterers and electricians at the same time. When the tongued and grooved sprung floor was being laid during Jan '60, we couldn't use the hall because of the dust inconvenience etc., but at least we knew the hall was nearly ready. After rehearsal, we went to the 'Rifle Volunteer', and the chat and decisions made during those lunchtimes were often more fulfilling than playing! The pub was on the corner with Tring Road, but has long since gone.

Opening night handbill – 1960.

The hall eventually opened on Saturday 12th March, 1960. The policy was to book a 'top' name every Saturday to appear live, for added attraction. On the opening night top recording singer Ronnie Carroll was booked to sing, using our band for his backing. With all of the 'stars' it was hoped they would turn up for rehearsal, but none ever did, making it very difficult for the band to support them. The one exception was the Vernon Girls vocal group, who arrived for a run through before 8.00pm.

The presentation of the band at 8.00pm that first evening was resplendent; with the Four Singing Aristocrats, Edwina and a well rehearsed band straining at the leash. I've suddenly mentioned the Singing Aristocrats, but that's how they seemed to be presented to us by the management at the Cali. They were an extremely well

Left The Four
Singing Aristocrats
giving their all with
Ray Miller &
Orchestra at the
California Pool
Ballroom, 1960.

Right Vocalist Edwina
Green about to take centre
stage at the 'Cali'.

rehearsed and experienced male vocal quartet, with their own orchestrations and a most amiable disposition. Their number was most definitely 'There's A Summer Place'.

Male vocal groups were 'in' at the time, such as the Four Preps, The Lettermen and The Four Aces etc. They sat with the band and sang with us for about 12 months, adding to the overall presentation of the band.

The excitement of the times is just a distant memory but one evening at the 'Cali' I'll never forget. The 'Queen' national anthem was always played at the end of each evening and everyone stood to attention, as the band rose to play it. Bill Lee (trumpet) was well over 6ft tall, and on cue stood up like a ramrod only to hit his head on a concrete beam, directly above him, which supported the overhead balcony. He was obviously badly concussed, and like the good trooper he was, kept blowing, producing every sort of note, except the right ones. He soon recovered, but needless to say, seating arrangements for the brass section were revised thereafter.

In those heady days, we were also to become 'film stars' for a while when the California Dance Hall was advertised during the interval at local cinemas by the Pearl and Dean advertisement newsreels, where the band was centrally featured throughout the advertisement.

We were soon to find out that the bane of our life was the 'taxman'! We had to make yearly returns to the tax office and they seemed to know exactly what you had earned. It was therefore important to declare reasonably accurate returns for peace of mind. Dad was the band's paymaster and demanded a signature from all the players he paid. This was not always popular, as some musicians tried to avoid paying tax – but not for long!

Even though the band was sounding excellent, Alex Brightman suggested that we should raise the standard even more by introducing top London musicians in key positions such as lead trumpet, tenor sax and lead alto sax. He made the first contact on our behalf, and we were ready to welcome (with some trepidation) into our ranks top London musicians. Trumpeter Brian Fielder was still playing with us, but unfortunately his lip 'kept cracking', which for a trumpeter was the worst thing, and he couldn't always reach the high notes and was often in pain. Brian therefore departed and was one of the first to be replaced by a London pro. Even so, Brian was with us during the formative years, and earned our respect for the genuine effort he had put in.

So on Sat 21st May, 1960 began the addition of some London 'corner' men for added spice. Sceptical we may have been, but the results were sensational, and introducing us to a succession of 'top pros' on that night were Frank Thornton (trumpet) and F. McGee. We had Frank to thank for suggesting we should buy the new Leeds Music 'Stage Band Series' of orchestration which did in fact further improve the overall presentation of the band.

Top session musicians were often free on a Friday or Saturday evening and were happy to nip down the newly opened M1 to play with us for £5 per engagement (we would be on anything from £1.5s.0d to £1.15s.0d.). The difference in the band

The Ray Miller Orchestra, 20th August 1960 at the California, now featured London professionals in the line-up. Rhythm Section l. to r.: Cecil Arnold (Piano); Stuart Goodyear (Snr) (Double Bass); David Johns (Drums). Saxophones l. to r.: Ken Hendley (2nd Alto); Syd Taylor (1st Alto); Syd Linton (Lead Tenor); Ken Tibbs (2nd Tenor) (partially hidden). Brass l. to r.: Keith Indge (2nd Trumpet); Frank Thornton (Lead Trumpet); Gordon Rushton (Trombone). Stuart Goodyear (Jnr) (Conducting/M.C.).

with 2 or 3 of them in the line up as lead tenor, alto sax or trumpet was electrifying. As soon as the first note was played, the crowd would turn to look.

It has to be remembered that the musical instruments through the 1940s, 50s and 60s that were at the forefront of popularity were the piano, trumpet, saxophone and trombone and even some of the exponents of the double bass and drums had international recognition. Their demise, however, was spectacular as the guitar gained in popularity with the 'pop' groups from the 1960s onwards.

I would now like to mention some of the top pros who played with us at the Cali, and at other venues over the years 1960–1963. Their style and confidence lifted the band, and there was no going back once the standard of performance had been set.

But first, the band of 'locals' who had filtered through one by one to join Dad, Ken Tibbs, David Johns and myself with a dedication and loyalty that had elevated us into the position we were now in:

Front/Leader	Yours Truly Stuart John Goodyear (Jnr)

Saxophones	Ken Tibbs (tenor)	
	Don Barrett (alto)	}
	Tom Lloyd (tenor)	}
	Ivor Pett (baritone)	}
	Frank Pipkin (alto)	}
	Peter Tasker (tenor)	} From
	Rory McGuinness (tenor)	}
	Ken Hendley (alto)	}
	Tony Britton (tenor)	}
	Stuart Byard (alto)	}
	Reg Harris (tenor)	}
	Stuart Horn (alto)	}
Brass	Billy Lee (trumpet)	}
	Roy Snape (trumpet)	}
	Keith Inge (trumpet)	}
	Eric Linney (trumpet)	}
	Brian Fielder (trumpet)	} From
	Eddie Houghton (trumpet)	}
	Don Excell (trombone)	}
	Nat Stone (trombone)	}
	Gordon Rushton (trombone)	}
	John Bridge (trombone)	}
Rhythm	David Johns (drums)	
	Stuart John Goodyear (Snr) (double bass)	
	Norman Thompson (Piano)	}
	Cecil Arnold (Piano)	} From
	Norman Wesley (Piano)	}

And now, the pros who were to form a very important part of the band, over the next year or two:

Jimmy Williams (alto sax)

Frank Thornton (trumpet with Peter Knight & Mantovani. Session Regular with Geoff Love, Stanley Black)

Grisha Farfel (trumpet with the Billy Cotton Showband and featured soloist on TV)

Dewi Jones (trumpet with Central Band, RAF Hillingdon)

Arnie Tweedie (trumpet)

Bob Efford (tenor sax with Ted Heath)
Moved to L.A.

Alex Hamilton (tenor sax with Central Band,
RAF Hillingdon)

Harry Pitch (trumpet & harmonica)

Ronnie Heasman (trumpet with Ted Heath)
– Owned garage & all musicians took
cars to him

Albert Hall (trumpet with Eric Delaney)

Alan Moorhouse (trumpet) Became famous
T.V. Music Director

Derek Abbott (trumpet with Johnny
Dankworth)

Syd Linton (tenor sax)

Duncan Campbell (trumpet with Ted Heath)

Roy Willox (alto with Ted Heath and
everyone!) Outstanding player

Syd Taylor (alto sax with Sidney Lipton &
Orchestra)

Harry Smith (alto sax)

Tommy Whittle (tenor sax) Britains most
famous!

Ronnie Simmons (trumpet with Ted Heath)

Stan Reynolds (trumpet) Leader with re-
formed Ted Heath Band

Alex McGregor (trumpet)

Harry Pitch was a celebrity in his own right, whose career to date has spanned five decades. During his first engagement with us on trumpet, we were pleasantly surprised when he alternated between trumpet and harmonica for his solos. His prowess on harmonica has made him world famous, as a soloist on movie sessions for Disney and Spielberg; for popular TV shows, most notably the BBC's "Last of the Summer Wine", and as backing for many hit records. He very recently (winter 2001) returned to Luton for a cabaret spot at the Pizza Express, Church Street – 40 years on from his first engagement with us – with return bookings offered there in 2002!

Grisha Farfel, solo trumpeter with the
Billy Cotton Band and T.V. star, gave
us his business card.

Trumpeter Harry Pitch became more
famous as a harmonica player.

Occasionally it was necessary to book a 'London' pianist if cabaret accompaniment or similar was required, and the two we could rely on were:

Trevor Williams (piano)

Jack Dove (piano)

With these guys, the band had reached its pinnacle.

Introducing them at the Cali, they continued to be an integral part of our line-up, wherever our services were required – whilst the 'big bands' were still in demand!!

Every Saturday was a frenzy of activity and packed houses, and some of the stars came and went, and we never even saw them, but we did support T.V. stars Ronnie Carroll and The Vernon Girls. Other stars to appear there at this time, and supported by their own groups, were Craig Douglas, Mark Wynter, Eden Kane and The Allisons, whose chart topper was "Are You Sure".

The two Saturdays that stand out though was when we shared the billing with Emile Ford and the Checkmates, & Tony Meehan and Jet Harris. They were so crowded you couldn't see an inch of the floor. Tony Meehan and Jet Harris left the famous 'Shadows' group, and had many top twenty hits as a duo, one of them being the 1940s number Besame Mucho which we also played most weeks.

CALIFORNIA POOL BALLROOM
WHIPSNADE ROAD, DUNSTABLE.

★ **YOUR EASTER HOLIDAY PROGRAMME** ★

THURSDAY APRIL 14th   "YOUR POP NIGHT"

Personal appearance of T.V. and Recording Star

CRAIG DOUGLAS

"Pretty Blue Eyes" and "Only Sixteen"

T.V. and Recording Stars	Newest Sensation
RUSS SAINTY	**BRET CONWAY**
and the	and
FABULOUS NU-NOTES	THE TEEN-BEATS
ADMISSION 6/6	8.0—11.30 p.m.

"YOUR SATURDAY DATE"

AN EXTRA SPECIAL SATURDAY PROGRAMME OF
NON-STOP DANCING

RAY MILLER	RUSS SAINTY
and His 13 Piece Orchestra	and the
with EDWINA GREEN	FABULOUS NU-NOTES
THE 4 SINGING ARISTOCRATS	
ADMISSION 5/6	8.0—12 p.m.

Grand Easter Monday Spectacular

Personal appearance of T.V. and Recording Stars
of the Goon Show

RAY ELLINGTON

AND HIS FAMOUS QUARTET
with all your Favourite Stars

RUSS SAINTY - THE NU-NOTES - PLUS! PLUS!

ADMISSION 6/6	8.0—12 p.m.
LICENSED BARS LATE EXTENSION —	LATE BUSES

Printed by L. Verby & Sons (TU) 172 Stoke Newington Rd. N.16

Easter Weekend handbill – 1960.

Right Another star of the 1960s, Eden Kane, on stage at the 'Cali'.

Below Signing copies of their latest release, 'The Allisons' at the California.

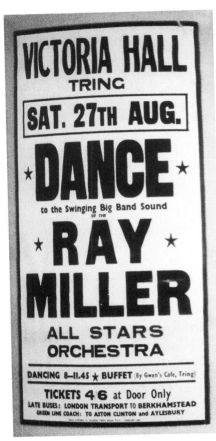

Out and about into Hertfordshire,
Tring 1960.

Wheathampstead, 1961.

Into 1961 at the 'Cali'.

As good as the residency at the 'Cali' was, it meant we were unable to play at the many venues that were making overtures regarding our availability, and the lads in the band also felt that a change of scenery now and again would rejuvenate their enthusiasm. So, by mutual agreement, the hall management and ourselves agreed that we could terminate our residency and share the bookings with other local dance bands. This arrangement continued well into 1962.

1961 — 1962

Compliments of the Season
from

california **★★★★** Pool
WHIPSNADE ROAD
Ballroom · Dunstable

Best wishes for a Merry Christmas and a Happy and Prosperous New Year

Thanking our Patrons for their support in the past years and assuring you of our best endeavours to dispense Happiness & Entertainment in the New Year

Wednesday, January 3rd. 7.30 till 10 p.m.
ADON WHITE BINGO CLUB.

Thursday, January 4th. 7 p.m. for 7.45 till 10 p.m.
International Wrestling. . . . .

Friday, January 5th, 8 p.m.
SCREAMING LORD SUCH AND THE SAVAGES.
THE JESTERS.

Saturday, January 6th, 8 p.m.
EMILE FORD AND THE CHECKMATES.
RAY MILLER ORCHESTRA.

BUILT on side of Dunstable Downs, used and named by the Ancient Britons CALIFORNIA, we provide all-the-year-round Recreation and Social Events for all ages every week as follows:—

Swimming. March till September.
Roller Skating. March till September.
Roller Hockey matches each Sunday afternoon.
Tuesday nights, Amateur Wrestling. 1/6. 7 p.m.
Wednesdays, Bingo. 2/6. 7.30 p.m.
Thursdays alternate weeks. Professional Wrestling.
Fridays, Rock-a-Cha-Cha. 8 p.m. 3/6.
Saturdays. Dancing non-stop. 6/6.
Sundays. Bingo. 2/6.

Various Rooms for hire from 15 to 1,000 for Dances, Banquets, Weddings.

Proprietors:
E. W. Green (Dunstable) Ltd.
Secretary: Miss P. Pugh.   Manager: Mr. Denis Allen.

Telephones: Box Office 62804. Foyer 62616:
· Filling Station, National Benzole, opens 7 a.m.

Printed by W. F. Bunker & Co., 26a, Chapel Street, Luton.

EMILE FORD & THE CHECKMATES
What Do You Want To Make Those Eyes At Me For?

In the late 50s and early 60s this group were in the UK charts for 87 weeks – 25 of those with 'What Do You Want To Make Those Eyes At Me For?'

Into 1962 at the 'Cali' and on the same bill as Emile Ford & the Checkmates.

The style of entertainment was rapidly changing by then, with soul and rock music being heavily promoted at the hall, which reflected the trend nation-wide. We were therefore happy to move on from the Cali, to venues where 'dance' music was still the order of the day. In little over 2 years we had come from novices to one of the town's top dance bands and were now playing at some of the halls that were revered by us in earlier years.

This was a most enjoyable period, and we were attracting large audiences at top 'out of town' venues such as Watford Town Hall, Bedford Corn Exchange and Harpenden Public Hall, and in Luton we were playing regularly at the Winter Assembly Hall, The George, Luton Technical College (Park Square) and Vauxhall Motors.

Above 1962 – St Albans.
Right 1963 – Bedford.

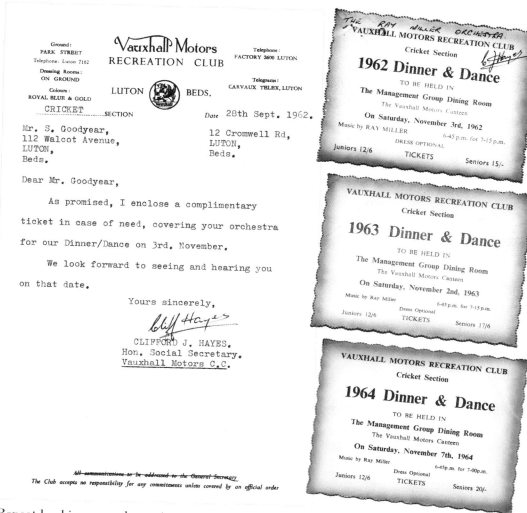

Repeat bookings were becoming commonplace – and good for business. Typical of many was from the Vauxhall Cricket Club. Note the Seniors admission for dinner & dance: 1962, 15/- (75p); 1963, 17/6 (87.5p); 1964, 20/- (£1.00). Our fee for the 1964 engagement was £15.00.

Left Promotional photograph taken for window display at Model Tailors, Dunstable Road, Luton. The band had ordered and taken delivery of new jackets, which were first worn at a Luton Technical College Dance, Park Square, on Saturday 18th February 1961. Musicians in background: Eddie Houghton (extreme left, Trumpet); Dewi Jones (Lead Trumpet); Ken Hendley (2nd Alto); Stuart Byard (Lead Alto, extreme right). Foreground, Proprietor of Model Tailors and Stuart Goodyear (Jnr).

Advertisement for Model Tailors & Model Modes.

The Chris Wand Band playing at the Winter Assembly Hall, Luton. (Typical 1950s scene). Note 'Jitterbugging Prohibited' sign to left of stage. Line-up l. to r.: Bill Bates (Piano); Ray Deakin (Trombone); Frank Creasey (Trumpet); Vernon Deakin (Trumpet, standing); Chris Wand (Drums); Harold Stott (2nd Alto Sax); Harry Kane (Lead Alto Sax); Mark Fischer (Tenor Sax); Dick Tomlinson (Double Bass) at rear.

During 1962 a new face arrived in Luton from Ossett, Yorkshire, who had been playing with the world famous John Barry Seven! Surely not, but yes, and pretty soon, Jimmy Stead's reputation as a brilliant tenor saxophonist was to be felt on the local music scene. Although our band was very settled, on one of our engagements at the George we needed a deputy and were fortunate enough to book Jimmy, whose performance left us with a lasting impression. Later, when we were in the throes of re-forming to a smaller combo, Jimmy would be the one we wanted as our versatile front liner. This was to be the case, and he became a close friend and irreplaceable member of the band.

The 'core' of the band was as young as the dancers, and we could feel when things were swinging and what the mood of the crowd was. Two of the venues, Watford Town Hall and The Winter Assembly Hall, Luton, displayed notices that stipulated 'No Jiving' and 'Jitterbugging Prohibited'.

At Watford it was to stop the girls' stiletto heels marking the floor, and at the Assembly Hall to avoid the possibility of the floor collapsing or moving due to unnecessary vibration etc., as the floor was built above the swimming bath for winter dancing. At the time it was like asking a crowd not to shout at a football match, because when 'up tempo' numbers were played, the natural tendency of the

The Frankie Turner Band at the Winter Assembly Hall, 1947. 'No Jitterbugging allowed' notice just visible to left of stage. Note another ex-Vauxhall orchestra music stand, centre stage.

dancers was to jive, and I can remember turning the 'No Jiving' sign on the stage round at Watford during one number, when the crowd was in full swing, much to the annoyance of the management, who ticked us off many times.

I have fond memories of Watford Town Hall, and the overall ambience of the place always brought the best out of us. Mambo Jambo was without doubt the most exhilarating number we played there, and always received a spontaneous ovation. But above all though, I remember when Cecil Arnold on piano played Chopin's Nocturne in E flat as a waltz, and the lights were dimmed as everyone took to the floor. Very moving and romantic.

Cecil also enjoyed the odd prank on stage and during one number left the piano to roll up each leg of Dad's trousers from behind, to his knees, in full view of the dancers, whilst he was still playing bass. The laugh was on Dad, but real musicians' humour.

Being young and impetuous did pay off though, because we were popular with the crowd and always attracted a full house, and it wasn't always the 'pros' that added the glitz either; out of the blue, trumpeter Keith Indge took it upon himself to take centre stage with the 'Trumpet Cha Cha' as a solo, which proved so popular with the band and dancers that it was always included in our repertoire. The number was in fact featured during my interview with Three Counties Radio in February 1995, documenting the history of the California Ballroom.

The Town Hall was completed in 1939 and stands at the main crossroads in the centre of the town. It is a simple, dignified and functional building. The architect was C. Cowles-Voysey

Below: The entrance to the two assembly halls which are part of the Town Hall. The main assembly hall seats 1,600 and is in constant use for concerts, dances, and a wide range of social functions. It has especially good acoustics and the main gramophone record companies use it regularly for recording purposes

WATFORD TOWN HALL

Entertainments & Catering Manager:
C. H. CARLTON-SMITH, M.I.M.E.

PROGRAMME OF EVENTS

MAY 1963

Programme of Events — Watford Town Hall — May, 1963

DAY	DATE	FUNCTION		TIME	PROMOTER	PRICE OF ADMISSION	TICKETS FROM
Wednesday	1st	London Philharmonic Concert	(For programme see over)	7.30 p.m.	London Philharmonic Orchestra	4/6 to 8/6	See over
Saturday	4th	Dance	The Debonaires Dance Orchestra	8 p.m.—12 mid.	Watford Corporation	5/-	At the door
Sunday	5th	Public Meeting and Entertainment	Parade from Harebreaks at 2.15 p.m. Speaker: Ian Mikardo	3 p.m.—5.30 p.m.	Watford May Day Committee	Free	—
Wednesday	8th	Wrestling Tournament		8 p.m.	Dale Martin Promotions Ltd.	3/6 to 10/-	Pickfords, Clarendon Road
Saturday	11th	Watford Music Festival Modern and Old Time	Junior Ballroom Competitions Peter Eames and His Music	2 p.m.—5.30 p.m.	Watford Music Festival	5/- in advance 6/- at the door	Irene Smythe, Rectory Lane, Rickmansworth, Tel. 5480
Saturday	11th	Dance	Freddie Maydwell and His Orchestra	8 p.m.—12 mid.	Watford Corporation	5/-	At the door
Wednesday	15th	Townswoman's Pantry	—	2 p.m.—4 p.m.	S.W. Herts Federation of Townswomen's Guilds	6d.	Guild Secretaries
Thursday	16th	Musicians Ball	Seven Bands	8 p.m.—1 a.m.	Watford Branch of the Musicians Union	5/-	Room 18 Town Hall
Friday	17th	Carnival Queen Dance (Old Time)	The Arcadians	8 p.m.—1 a.m.	Watford Borough Carnival Fund	6/6	Mrs. Higgs, 85 Durban Road Wat. 21990
Saturday	18th	Dance	Ray Miller and His Orchestra	8 p.m.—12 mid.	Watford Corporation	5/-	At the door
Tuesday	21st	Social Evening	Alex Miller and His Band	7.30 p.m.—12 mid.	St. Albans and District L.V. Domino League	5/-	Blacksmiths Arms, St. Peters Street, St. Albans.
Wednesday	22nd	Wrestling Tournament	—	8 p.m.	Dale Martin Promotions Ltd.	3/6 to 10/-	Pickfords, Clarendon Road
Thursday	23rd	Hallé Orchestra	(For programme see over)	7.30 p.m.	Hallé Concerts Society	4/6 to 10/6	See over
Saturday	25th	Dance	The Commanders	8 p.m.—12 mid.	Watford Corporation	5/-	At the door
Sunday	26th	Commonwealth Youth Sunday Service	Young People and Adults Welcome	3 p.m.	Watford Youth Committee	Free	—
Monday	27th	Mayor Making Ceremony		3 p.m.		Free	Town Hall
Friday	31st	Biennial Conference	Public Meeting	7.30 p.m.	South England Conference of Seventh-Day Adventists	Free	
Saturday June 1st		Biennial Conference	—	9 a.m.—5 p.m.	South England Conference of Seventh-Day Adventists	—	—

THIS INFORMATION IS GIVEN FOR THE CONVENIENCE OF THE PUBLIC
THE WATFORD CORPORATION CAN GIVE NO GUARANTEE THAT ANY FUNCTION WILL TAKE PLACE ON THE DATE SHOWN

Left above Many of our 'better' performances were at the Watford Town Hall. Posters were displayed on the walls between the doors and I always looked forward to the interval drink at 'The Horns' (the pub next door), where we mingled and chatted to the dancers.

Left below It was good to be included in the Watford Town Hall 'programme of events'.

TOWN HALL WATFORD

DO YOU ENJOY

DANCING

THEN JOIN

RAY MILLER AND HIS ORCHESTRA

8 p.m. to 12 midnight

Saturday, 21st November

ADMISSION 5/- AT THE DOOR

DANCING IS INDEED A REAL JOY AND PLEASURE AT THE TOWN HALL WATFORD EVERY SATURDAY. SOMEBODY WILL BE WAITING TO MEET YOU DANCING

St. Valentine's Eve

MODERN BALLROOM DANCE

SATURDAY 13th FEBRUARY

8 P.M. – MIDNIGHT

IN THE

OVALTINE BALLROOM

WITH

RAY MILLER and HIS ORCHESTRA

5/-

OVALTINE SOCIAL CLUB

Above 1964, and still doing it at Watford Town Hall. Making a rare appearance with us, accomplished pianist Derek Chance, who was a personnel officer at Electrolux, played on this engagement.

Left 1965, and it was always a joy to play in the beautiful Ovaltine Factory Ballroom at Kings Langley, near Hemel Hempstead.

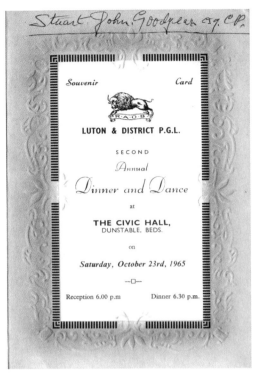

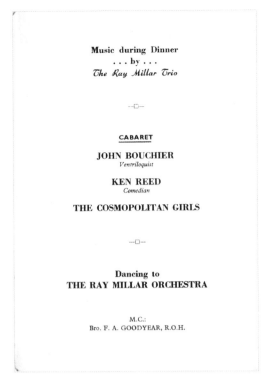

Stuart Goodyear (Snr) played for the 'Buffaloes' in 1937 – our turn in 1965 and 1974. *Above* Civic Hall, Dunstable – 1965. *Below* Winston Churchill, Dunstable – 1974.

G.L.E.

DOVE LODGE
No. 8210

takes pleasure in presenting a

Dinner & Dance

THE WINSTON CHURCHILL
DUNSTABLE BEDS

SATURDAY 18th MAY 1974

Reception 6.30p.m.   Dinner 7.00p.m.

Toasts

H.M. THE QUEEN
Proposed by The Chairman
W. Davies, R.O.H.

THE LADIES AND GUESTS
Proposed by Bro. T. Harrington, C.P.
Reply by Mrs. M. A. Barrows

ABSENT BRETHREN
Proposed by Bro. R. Costall, K.O.M.

Dancing to
"THE RAY MILLER BAND"

Yours truly and Keith Indge at David Johns' and Jeane's wedding reception at the George Hotel on Saturday 18th May 1963. Pianist and trumpeter at a drummer's wedding! (Wonder what the topic of conversation would have been).

Competition for bookings was becoming difficult, as more and more dance halls were turning to 'pop' or closing, and events unfolding in the band were also contributing to the inevitable restructuring of the band.

Ken Tibbs, being married, was ready for less commitment and wanted to switch from tenor sax to piano, so in 1962 left to form his own quartet, with drummer Dave Bousted, which was called the Ken Davey Four, and kept a busy diary for 9 years. Singing with the band was Dick Chamberlain, who was following in the footsteps of his father Joe, who sang with the Len Bolton Orchestra at the George Hotel. Dick also sang with the Victors pop group.

David's career (away from our band) was beginning to take off, and having met his Jeane at my 21st at the Somerset Tavern, married her in May 1963. Mum attended David's wedding, which was probably the last function she attended in good health, as she was soon to be diagnosed with cancer. Margaret and I married in January 1964 which she again attended, but was in very poor health. Thankfully she saw the band in full swing before her untimely death on 25th March 1964, aged 52.

Big band engagements were now getting fewer, but David would still make the effort to play from wherever in the country he was based. In all probability, and so very satisfying, the very last big band we put out was for my Uncle Aub (Dad's brother Francis) who was the Mayor of Luton in 1965/66, and we played for his Ball at the George Hotel in May 1965. David never played after that and was soon to go to America to seek his fortune. The George was soon to close also.

Above The days of the big dance band were drawing to a close, but Vauxhall kept to tradition at Christmas 1964.

Below Invitation to the Mayor's Ball – 1965, held at the Luton College of Technology.

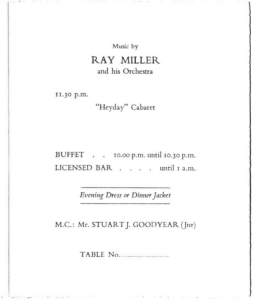

Terry Hammond and the Fiesta Four at the California Ballroom (c.1961), running through a number with a young lady vocalist, who was auditioning for work. This stage area was at the opposite end of the hall to the larger main stage. Band personnel l. to r.: Derek Hunt (lead Guitar/Vocals); Laurie Jeffs (Bass Guitar); John Brack (Drums); Tony Reynolds (Rhythm Guitar). Within the next couple of years, John, Derek and Tony joined my re-formed band, and gave us the added dimension needed for the rapidly changing music scene.

It left Dad and myself in charge, and as big bands in general had 'had' their day, it was an opportune time for a major rethink. We still had bookings to fulfil, and had unfortunately entered a period where many different players were booked on a weekly basis. This caused Dad and me a lot of last minute running around and often took the enjoyment out of the evening's engagement.

A regular drummer was the immediate priority, who was proficient both at ballroom and 'pop'. Our introduction to John Brack was fortuitous, not so much that he took on the mantle of 'new' drummer, but because he introduced us to two of his friends who were to play a significant role in determining the line-up of the Ray Miller Band for the next 20 years. Although they were both guitarists, Derek Hunt and Tony Reynolds gave us the spice needed to suit the mood of the day.

The three were part of the Terry Hammond Four, with Derek as lead guitar/vocalist and Tony on rhythm guitar. They blended in perfectly with one or two saxes, and I realised that 'at a stroke' the band, augmented by Derek and Tony, who were able to play dance music as well as 'pop' in the latest idiom, would give us the ability to cater for the broader section of age group, who were now attending Social and Working Men's clubs and Dinner Dances in ever increasing numbers. The Terry Hammond Four had also made their mark at the California Ballroom, and often shared the evening with Russ Sainty and Rhett Stoller, but their claim to fame

Derek Hunt, typical of the many young men on the 1960s 'Pop' scene, as he was before he became our dance band lead guitar/vocalist. Derek is now a dedicated keyboard player and composer, at his Caddington home.

was supporting recording star Johnny Duncan and The Blue Grass Boys at Garston Community Centre. It was a bold, if not unusual step to take, as there was a certain amount of animosity between the 'old bands' and the 'new groups', but all concerned enjoyed the marriage and for Dad and me, a settled and busy band was good news. So there you are, if you can't beat 'em, join 'em, and in doing so, we secured the immediate way forward, but the band was unrecognisable from the one just a year earlier.

Vauxhall Motors Recreation Club - Luton Social Section
PRESENTS

SPECIAL MODERN SPORTS DAY CARNIVAL

DANCE
IN THE

STAFF DINING ROOM
ON

SATURDAY, 13th JUNE, 1964

8 p.m. to Midnight   Doors Open 7.30 p.m.

Dancing to the rhythm of the

RAY MILLER BAND
(12 Piece)
Featuring LONDON ARTISTES : With DEREK HUNT as vocalist
M.Cs.: Arthur Petty and Geoff. Noble

Supported by

THE CLARIONS
VOCAL ACCORDIAN GROUP
(From B.B.C.1 Blue Peter Programme)

Tickets can be obtained from your
AREA COMMITTEE MEMBERS 👉
TICKETS 6/- EACH
NO TICKETS WILL BE SOLD AT THE DOOR

Also from
Members of SPORTS SPECTACULAR
LUTON AND DUNSTABLE RE
AND CANTEEN

Admission to the Bar for visitors to be Membership
Card only. Temporary Membership Cards may be

Rights of Admission Rese

Spot Prizes   :   :   Balloons   :   :
Admittance by Main Entrance to Staff Dining Room (Opposite Car Park)
LATE COACHES (Luton and Dunstable) FARE 2 -

Come along and bring al

Left 1964, Vauxhall Motors Sports Day Dance, with Derek Hunt as featured vocalist. Also on the bill were The Clarions, who had just made a TV appearance on BBC's 'Blue Peter'.

CALIFORNIA POOL BALLROOM

WHIPSNADE ROAD, DUNSTABLE   Telephone 214

FRIDAY, AUG 12th.   "ROCK-A-CHA-CHA NIGHT"
Special Engagement of
JOHN CHAPMAN, England's most versatile organist.
TERRY HAMMOND and the **FIESTA FOUR**.
Also
SIR ANTHONY BARRON with the Stupendous "Barron" Knights.
8 till 11.30.   Adm. 3/6.   Late extension.   Late buses.

SAT., AUG. 13th.   Your "SATURDAY NIGHT DATE"
8—12. Return of **RAY MILLER** with a special 13-piece orchestra. Also **TERRY HAMMOND** and the **FIESTA FOUR**. Adm. 6/6. Late extension. Late buses to Luton and Leighton Buzzard.

MON., AUG. 15th.   "CALIFORNIA JAZZ CELLAR"
with the **LEASIDE SEVEN**. Informal atmosphere. 8 till 11 p.m. Admission 2/6. Licensed table service.

WED., AUG. 17th.   "OLD-TIME DANCING"
8 till 11 p.m. Admission 3/6. With the versatile organist, **JOHN CHAPMAN**, and M.Cs. **Mr. and Mrs. J. West.**

Right All the locals on parade in this advert for the Cali, August 1960. Terry Hammond; The Leaside Seven; Ray Miller.

Dad, on double bass, at 'home', and settled with The Steve Baker trio at the Co-operative employees' Social Club in Stockingstone Road, Luton (c. mid 1970s) with his old mate Billy Coomber on piano, and Tony Baker on drums.

Dad was restless; we were not playing his style of music, and also the double bass was perhaps out of place, especially as we now had Tony Reynolds who was an excellent rhythm guitarist, who easily blended in with sax of the day Mark Fischer or Ken Hendley. It didn't take long for him to move on, and he joined an old friend and excellent pianist, Billy Coomber, plus Tony 'Brusher' Baker (a close friend of mine at Vauxhall) on drums, to form the Steve Baker Band. On saxes would be Les Old (alto) and Keith Shury (tenor sax). Les lived next to us at 110 Walcot Avenue, and whether or not we influenced him, at 11 years old he decided to learn alto sax, and Dad introduced him to Stuart Byard who gave him lessons, and he was to become proficient enough to team up with Keith Shury on tenor to form the band's front line. Ken Hendley would also play for the band, who was becoming known in the town as a good versatile player, who would willingly play for anyone, if available. Dave Long later became their sax player. Dad saw out his playing days with Billy, and both played well into their 70s, with the Naval Club in Crawley Green Road, the Co-op Employees Social Club in Stockingstone Road, and Oxen Road Club being their most prolific venues.

Dad would often turn his hand to songwriting, purely for his own satisfaction, and tried really hard to pen a 'winner' for Christmas over many years. He wrote many, but couldn't hit that 'something special', I suspect because his style was stuck in the 1930s idiom, none more than one he wrote when Mum died in 1964.

The Steve Baker Quartet with Les Old on sax.

Back to the band, and it was becoming evident that drummer John Brack would be happier playing with pop groups and Irish style show bands, and didn't really enjoy mixing it with strict tempo, so he left to join another group, at the earliest opportunity. It was opportune because the George Hotel had just closed, and I was quick to employ Jerry Blain as my permanent drummer. It would mean though being a taxi driver (for the next 10 years) as Jerry didn't drive.

I was witnessing at first hand the emergence of the pop scene and the associated guitar/vocal 'groups', which were to become dominant at a majority of dances, and of course very popular with the younger set. At many dances, we were booked to share the stage with one of them, giving the dancers the best of both worlds.

WHEN I LOST YOU.

VERSE.

ALL HEARTS ARE LIGHTER IN SUMMERTIME,
ALL THE WORLD IS IN TUNE.
ALL THINGS ARE BRIGHTER IN SUMMERTIME,
LOVERS HAPPILY CROON.
BUT FOR ME,
SUMMER BRINGS A SAD MEMORY.

CHORUS.

I LOST THE SUNSHINE AND ROSES,
I LOST THE HEAVEN'S SO BLUE,
I LOST THE BEAUTIFUL SPRINGTIME,
I LOST A ROSE IN YOU,
I LOST THE ANGEL WHO GAVE ME,
SUMMER THE WHOLE WINTER THROUGH,
I LOST THE GLADNESS
THAT TURNED INTO SADNESS,
WHEN I LOST YOU.

Left **When Mum died in 1964, Dad wrote these lyrics. (Musical accompaniment lost unfortunately).**

The George, Etcetera

Now is the ideal time to dedicate a special mention to Luton's favourite venue, the George Hotel, and the many related tales and memories it conjures up. The 'George', as it was affectionately known, was situated in George St., Luton, and was without doubt the most stable and prestigious dance venue in Luton until its closure in the 1960s. Most bands would get great satisfaction from playing there, and even 'off duty' musicians would enjoy meeting in one of the two men's bars for their night off.

The monthly 'What's On' Magazine.

Geoff Stokes and his band at the George Hotel, 1944. Geoff is seen standing with clarinet and the line-up includes Jimmy Iremonger on guitar and Billy Seaford on piano. This was Geoff Stokes' first big band; prior to this he ran a quintet.

Well connected bass player Derek Maurice Impey takes to the stage at the George Hotel in the early 1950s, with his new band, which he called the Derek Maurice Band! The line-up featured many well known regulars, with notably Dick Tomlinson (Double Bass) and Diana Godfrey (Vocals). Derek is standing centre stage, wearing light-coloured jacket.

I started going to the George in 1957, where Ken Green was the resident band on Thursdays and Saturdays. It was very popular and I can remember so many things as if it were yesterday:

The beautiful Lounge Bar, which was used by the lads for that 'special' date etc.

The dance hall attracted many American servicemen, and, if any of the local girls danced with them, they were unfairly called Yankee Bashers by the local lads.

When the Cha Cha Cha was at the height of its popularity (approx. 1960) the girls would dance in one continuous line and in perfect step. Unforgettable stuff, to which the band responded with a non-stop selection of numbers such as 'Patricia'; 'Tea For Two'; 'Wheels'; 'That Old Feeling' & 'Makin'-Whopee' etc. (Many standards were played in Cha Cha Cha tempo).

The superb band, which included so many of the best local musicians I was getting to know very well.

Well, that's how I remember the George, but it had a longer history than I can recollect, so I called on drummer John 'Jerry' Blain (who joined my band when the George closed) and Ron Franks (piano) to recall a few of the characters and stories associated with it during its hey-day.

Advertisements for the George Hotel c.1960. Note hire of ballroom and bar, 15 guineas.

The Barry Austyn Orchestra at the 'George', and playing what appears to be the Gay Gordons, with Brian Sapwell (Trumpet) and George Ashby (Trombone) leading the fun, and drummer Basil Osman enjoying the frolics. Saxophones from l. to r.: John Murray (Alto Sax); Jackie Morrison (Alto Sax); Stan Tisbury (Tenor Sax); Brian Arnall (Tenor Sax) (stage may be temporary position, opposite main stage).

Looks like John Murray enjoyed a Manns Brown Ale! – at the George. (Note box compartment on stand for cigarettes etc.)

The stuff that dreams are made of! Our band at the George Hotel, Friday 28th April 1961.
Line-up: Rhythm section: Norman Thompson (Piano); David Johns (Drums); Stuart
Goodyear (Snr) (Double Bass). Saxophones l. to r.: Ken Hendley (2nd Alto); Stuart Byard
(lead Alto); Tommy Whittle (lead Tenor); Ken Tibbs (2nd Tenor). Brass: Keith Indge (2nd
Trumpet); Grisha Farfel (lead Trumpet); John Bridge (Trombone) out of picture; Yours
truly (fronting/M.C.). Apart from playing at the George, we were thrilled to have top
international recording stars Tommy Whittle and Grisha Farfel, in the line-up. Before
coming to Luton, Scotsman Norman Thompson used to play with the famous Clyde
Valley Stompers.

To touch on Jerry's musical career will give a brief insight into the musicians of
the George, which was closely entwined with a succession of bands from the
1940s until it closed. Jerry's introduction to music was when his dad took him to
Luton Town F.C., where there was a Military Marching Band on show, and he was
immediately attracted to the drums. The rest is history.

I will always be indebted to Jerry, who taught me the precise tempos and
rhythms, which were so necessary when we started playing for larger and more
sophisticated audiences. So much so, that we were to become very much in
demand for strict tempo dances.

So, going back to the 1930s, the band who kept dancers entertained was Wesley
Lee and the St. Louis players. They would play at a Flannel Dance (casual) or a
Select Dance (Jacket & Tie) for an adoring public right up to 1940.

Same function and line-up as previous photograph, but gives opportunity to mention trombonist John Bridge (nearest camera) from Watford, who became a good friend and a regular member over many years.

WESLEY LEE AND HIS
THE NEW St LOUIS PLAYERS DANCE ORCHESTRA

Pictured here in 1934, Wesley Lee and his "The New St. Louis Players' Dance Orchestra" were regulars at the George Hotel Ballroom. Personnel l. to r.: Jim Hyde (Trumpet); Leo Dawson (Double Bass); Alec Gibbons (Trumpet); Geoff Stokes (Sax & Clarinet); Wesley Lee (Drums); Bill Hayward (Sax & Clarinet); Syd Hawkes (Piano); Bob 'Gunner' Stokes (Sax & Clarinet). Bob & Geoff were brothers. Seeing the line-up of instruments, many of the band were multi-talented, and would switch to clarinet, alto sax, tenor sax, baritone sax, saxophone or accordion as required. Note also, no music!

Wesley Lee and his band (1943), with Wesley (standing centre stage), M.C. Barnes Evans (standing next to piano) and vocalist Joan Hunter Reed, all sporting carnations. Line-up of band members: Spence Bell (Piano); Frank Reid (Double Bass); Chris Wand (Drums); saxophones l. to r.: Cecil Capon (2nd Alto); Vince Shepherd (Tenor & Baritone); Gordon Buckley (Lead Alto); Eric Slaney (Tenor); George Wilkinson (Trombone); Bert Poulton (Trumpet) on left; centre unknown.

Bass player (and paint salesman) Dick Tomlinson with his Blue Shadows followed with a short residency, then (approx.) 1940 saw another change, when Burton Gillis and his orchestra took centre stage. Pianist Ron 'Waffle' Franks was able to relate in detail, with his first hand knowledge, Burton's time at The George as follows:

Approx. at the outbreak of war, Ron was playing with his first band Fred Janes, resident at Dunstable Town Hall, and also included Charlie Goss (alto sax); also sharing piano duties with Ron was Bill Harris. Ron worked at George Kent's, Luton, along with a great many other local musicians, and worked close to saxophonist Vince Shepherd who was already a member of Burton Gillis's Orchestra. Vince was very tall, with a sombre gait, hence being nicknamed an 'undertakers clerk' by his associates.

Burton Gillis took a booking at the Connaught Rooms, Upper George Street, above Arthur Day's Music Shop, but needed a pianist and it was Vince who approached Ron to take the booking, which he was pleased to do. He must have impressed because he was asked to join Burton Gillis at The George, due to the departure of pianist Bill Bates who had left to join the Navy. Furthermore, did he know of an alto sax, as one was also required in the band? Charlie Goss was an obvious candidate, who, when asked, jumped at the opportunity. Fred Janes was upset by the departure of two of his key men, and promptly packed in his residency, which was taken over by Ron 'Nibble' Perrins. Fred Janes ran the Embassy Band.

Burton Gillis was a top London musician and played with Billy Cotton and Henry Hall before coming to Luton, to open a grocery/confectioners corner shop on the Dunstable Road, opposite Beechwood Road.

Burton Gillis and his band at the George Hotel Ballroom, Feb 1941. L. to r.: Vernon Critten (Double Bass); Len 'Sugar' Tate (Guitar); Tommy Lewtas (Drums); Vince Shepherd (Alto Sax); Bill Bates (Piano); Gordon Buckley (Baritone Sax); Unknown (Tenor Sax); Burton Gillis (Alto Sax, leader). Gwen Haynes was regularly booked as vocalist and occasionally Doris Duggan.

His first engagements in Luton were at the Kingsway Tavern, but he was soon to become in demand at The George, where he led his band on clarinet (doubling sax) for many years. He was able to arrange his own band parts, and, such was his ability, often turned an arrangement out during an interval, which required a great understanding with the men around him. A popular member of the band was guitar/vocalist Len 'Sugar' Tate (Tates Forms & Printers), whose ability and charisma when performing the 'latest' numbers made him a personality in his own right.

Burton's band won national band contests, but, having won their way to a 'National' final one year, he died suddenly, before the event.

Burton also gave Sunday wartime concerts at Golders Green. Incidentally, when I phoned 77 year old freelance photographer Cliff Hawkins (who had retired to Christchurch) to clarify some details, he spoke at some length of his memories of the superb Burton Gillis at the George, and also Burton's Sunday night concerts at the Alma Theatre.

Jerry Blain's brother Frank took music lessons with Burton, and was also destined to become a popular and well-respected tenor saxophonist in the local dance band circuit. At 16, Jerry joined an accordion band called the 5 Aces. A year later in 1939,

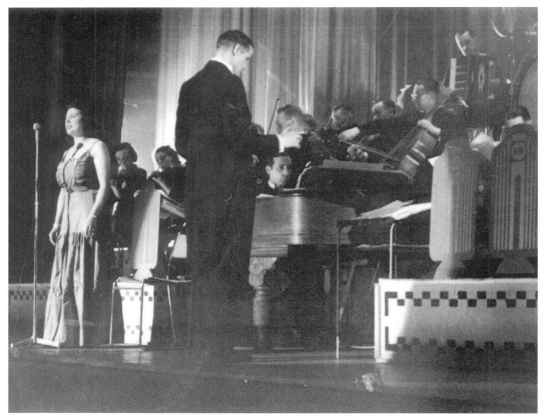

"The Union" was also a popular concert venue, and shown singing there in January 1941 is Barbara Bird, supported by the Vauxhall Orchestra conducted by Fred Green, with Jack Yeomans on the piano. Note the bandstands in shape of Vauxhall front grille, with 'VM'.

he took employment at George Kent's in Biscot Road, Luton, which was renowned for the many musicians working there, and they even had their own brass band. In fact, Jerry often lent the band his bass drum for use on many engagements.

Jerry became friends with Sid Hawkes, a Gauge Checker and (more importantly) an excellent pianist, and Lancashire lad Len Bolton, a Grinding Machine Operator who was a superb trumpeter. They teamed up and became popular as the Len Bolton trio, but were soon to augment to a larger band (including the introduction of Mark Fischer) to become established as one of the Town's best ever dance orchestras, following the standard already set by Burton Gillis. Mark in fact joined in 1944 when the band were regulars at the 'George' until the late '40s.

Len Bolton was very much his own man and was prone to dismissing musicians when it suited him, and on one such occasion dismissed Ron Franks to replace him with Derek Chance. Another pianist who also played with Len Bolton was Harold 'Schub' Stanton who not only played sax but was also an excellent arranger and did many scores for the famous Ray Martin and His Orchestra.

The Len Bolton Orchestra were in great demand at this time, and played regular

The Len Bolton Orchestra at the George. Line-up l. to r.: Syd Hawkes (Piano); Frank Bolton – Len's brother (Double Bass); (Guitar); (Trombone); Joe Chamberlain (Vocals); John 'Jerry' Blain (Drums); Len Bolton (leader/Trumpet); Harry Kane (lead Alto); Norman Cardell (2nd Alto); Danny McDiarmid (Tenor Sax).

Sunday concerts held at the Union (later the Ritz) cinema in Gordon Street. Mark remembers playing at the Hammersmith Palais, The Film Ball at the Guildhall Cambridge (attended by Richard Attenborough and Jean Kent) and the SKF 50th year Anniversary Ball at the Savoy Hotel, London, as three of their most memorable functions.

I was never fortunate enough to see the Len Bolton Orchestra, but in later years played, and became great friends, with many of his "stars". Amongst them were: Frank Blain, Eric Slaney and Mark Fischer (tenor saxes); Billy Seaford, Jim Smith (boy, could he swing), Dave Wildman and Ron Franks (pianists); George Ashby (trumpet & trombone); Charlie Goss (alto sax). Joe Chamberlain was their singer, but he was also busy away from the orchestra, notably at the Alma concert evenings where he used the stage name Alan Cole.

Seeing Dave Wildman's name reminds me of the early Rainbow Melody Makers when his daughter Marilyn was actually learning some of our numbers with the intention of singing with the band, and I used to go to the Wildmans' house, early in 1958, at 69 Liverpool Road, Luton to run through them with her on Dave's beautiful grand piano. We did get a repertoire together and she sang with us at the Trade Union Club, Church Street, but was offered a summer season at Westgate-On-Sea, Kent, and that was that! One of her numbers, 'For There's A Fire Down Below (Down Below In My Heart)', was a showstopper, which was incidentally the

1958, and Marilyn Wildman was off to a Summer season. Crooning with a dance band indeed!

JOHN WADE . . . an up and coming Comedy Magician who began his career by Conjuring to his schoolfellows. Appeared in Pantomime, as Simple Simon, this year for the first time with much success. Apart from his own acts of slick magic, he is an able compere and feed.

MARILYN WILDMAN . . . this vivacious young Soubrette has crowded a wealth of experience into a busy career. Summer seasons at Worthing, Exmouth and Minehead, and principal girl in three Pantomimes. During the Winter she has been crooning with a Dance Orchestra.

very first number arranged for the band by Ken Tibbs.

Jerry was about to complete his national service (1946–48) and joined Len Bolton at the George when he was demobbed. Len Bolton departed the Town to play in Billy Smart's Circus Band but returned shortly after to front Frankie Turner's Band for a while, before emigrating to Australia.

Towards the end of the war, drummer Teddy Dobbs, who had been running a

The Frankie Turner Band at the George, 1942/3. Line-up l. to r.: Ron Franks (Piano); Len Bolton (fronted band on Trumpet); Jack Winch (Bass); Frankie Turner (leader/Alto); Jackie Morrison (Alto Sax); Keith Burgoine (Drums); Derek Wheldon (Tenor Sax); Cliff Cox (Guitar); Brian Barton (Tenor Sax).

band on Clacton Pier, came to Luton, to try his luck at the George. To fill his newly formed band, Teddy auditioned for players at Beech Hill Conservative Club, and amongst those to be chosen were Frank Reid (double bass), George Ashby (trumpet), Frank Turner (alto sax) and George Wilkinson (trombone). For whatever reason, Teddy only lasted for a few engagements.

Pianist Spence Bell and bass player Frank Reid 'stood out in a crowd' when they played in the same rhythm section together at the George or the Grand Theatre, Waller Street, as Spence's head leaned to the left and Frank's to the right, a characteristic they both had from birth, and had to withstand many a leg-pull throughout their careers. More often, at the Grand, drummer Jack Collier and double bass Vernon Critten (Snr) would be on duty with Spence, but dodging the plum and cherry stones lobbed down from the upper circle was a regular hazard.

Frank 'Hacker' Reid was a long established musician in town, and earlier in his career played sousaphone/bass with the Sidney Phasey pit orchestra at the Alma theatre.

The Frankie Turner Band was another top local band in the 1940s, which also played regularly at The George, with a short residency approx. 1943. Amongst those playing with the band were Keith Burgoine (drums) and Ken Green (2nd trumpet). Ken, using this as a platform and always being the entrepreneur, decided to form his own band, which was destined to become the resident band at The George for many years.

Geoff Stokes and his Band at the Cresta (c.1960), but for years was almost resident at Harpenden Public Hall. Line-up: Derek Tearle, Agent/Manager (standing at Piano); rhythm section: Tom Stark (Piano); Jack Stone (D/Bass); Keith Burgoine (Drums); brass section l. to r.: Ray Deakin (Trombone); Brian Sapwell (Trumpet); Jim Bull (Trumpet); saxophones: Eric Slaney (Tenor Sax); Dave Bradley (Tenor Sax); Charlie Goss (Alto Sax); Geoff Stokes (Alto Sax).

Keith became a good friend of mine, and was a real character, always good for a laugh. He was a life long friend of Jerry and went on to join the Geoff Stokes Orchestra. Keith ran the Mill End Nursery on the Harlington Road, Sharpenhoe, which Margaret and I often visited, both for plants and an enjoyable run out and chat. Keith's son Martin, now runs the nursery. Whenever I went to the Harpenden Public Hall, Geoff Stokes would inevitably be the band, and Keith's upright profile and driving enthusiasm was always evident. Geoff (lead alto sax) and his brother Bob Stokes (lead tenor sax) grew up with dad, and I always enjoyed the 'light-hearted' presentation of the band, which was enhanced by the antics of trumpeter Jim Bull who often played his valve trombone for a bit of extra fun, after donning a ginger wig!

Ken Green and his orchestra was the band I remember with affection, and was resident at the 'George' whilst it remained a Public Dance Hall. The line-up of Ken's band that I fondly remember was Norman Wesley (piano); Derek Impey (bass); Jerry Blain (drums); Mark Fischer & Frank Blain (tenor saxes); Harry Kane & Gordon Buckley (alto saxes); Reg Harris (baritone sax & poss., tenor); or Vince Shepherd (baritone sax) and then John Lambert (baritone); Ken Green

Ken Green and his Dance Orchestra – 1950s. Line-up l. to r.: Ken Green (leader/Trumpet);
Norman Wesley (Piano); Dick Kirk (Trumpet); Vince Shepherd (2nd Alto Sax); Jerry Blain
(Drums); Gordon Buckley (lead Alto); Derek Impey (Bass); Frank Blain (lead Tenor Sax);
Reg Harris (2nd Tenor Sax).

Ken Green and his Dance Orchestra at the George, sporting summer jackets. Personnel:
back row l. to r.: Jerry Blain (Drums); Derek Impey (Bass); Norman Wesley (Piano); front
l. to r.: Ken Green (Trumpet); Dick Kirk (Trumpet); Vince Shepherd (2nd Alto Sax);
Gordon Buckley (lead Alto); Frank Blain (Tenor Sax).

This time at the Winter Assembly Hall, and enjoying himself, Ken Green puts his orchestra through its paces, (1950s). Line-up l. to r.: Ken Green (Leader); Norman Wesley (Piano); Dick Kirk (Trumpet); Vince Shepherd (2nd Alto Sax); Gordon Buckley (lead Alto); John 'Jerry' Blain (Drums); Frank Blain (lead Tenor Sax); Derek Impey (Double Bass); Reg Harris (2nd Tenor); Diana Godfrey (née Raggatt) (Vocals).

(leader/trumpet) accompanied by either Vernon Deakin or Bill Lee (trumpet); Ray Deakin or George Wilkinson (trombone). Diana Raggatt was on vocals, and Barnes Evans took on the duties of M.C. quite regularly. Mark Fischer joined Ken Green full time in 1959, after leaving the Carlton Orchestra.

Also worth a mention at this stage is local lad Reggie Goff who was a brilliant singer and alto sax/clarinet player, who played with all the best local bands during the late 1930s and 1940s, before becoming an international recording star in his own right. Born in Gosport in 1915, Reggie lived with his parents in Blenheim Crescent, Luton during his formative years. Although Reggie was in a wheelchair, it did not impair his versatility, and his career took off in 1939 when he joined the BBC Dance Orchestra, directed by Billy Ternent, as lead alto, and stayed with the band until 1946, which by then was led by Stanley Black.

Reggie formed his own band, which he maintained continuously until his death in 1956 at Hereford, but became a household name as a popular vocalist with hits on both sides of the Atlantic for Decca records, some of which were only recorded for the American market. Cyril Stapleton's Orchestra supplied most of the accompaniments, but the Felix King and Ted Heath bands also supported him over the years.

For a while, his trio played at the Wilbury Hotel, Letchworth, with Jerry Blain on drums and Darky Wilson on piano, and would you believe, whilst I was writing this, Three Counties Radio played Reggie singing 'Moon Above Malaya', accompanied by the Roland Peachey Orchestra!

Certainly my night at The George was a Thursday, not necessarily for dancing, but certainly to meet my mates, and most definitely to listen to the music. After strolling the town, I guess I would enter The George usually just before the interval, so as to chat to the musicians during their break. Funny how things stick in your mind, but whenever I popped my head into the dance hall (about 9.45pm) Ken's band would always be playing a number called La Mulata Rumbera!

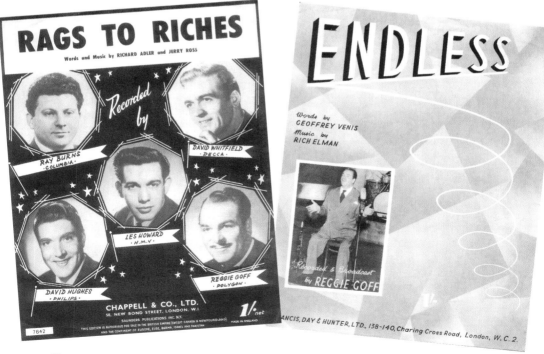

Rags to Riches – Reggie Goff.

Endless – Reggie Goff (Sheet Music – 1954).

Left My night at the George was Thursday, and as tickets were torn in half upon admission, a complete ticket like this would be a rare possession.

Right Ken Green always included a good share of Latin American numbers for the dancers at the George; the Rumba 'La Mulata Rumbera' was one of my favourites.

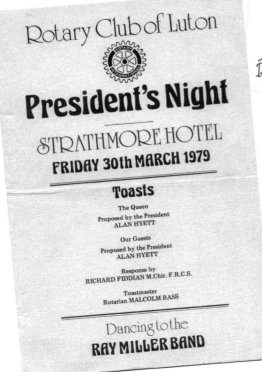

Left 1979 – Mustn't forget the Strathmore Hotel, Luton. Local 'vet' Alan Hyett had a busy President's night.

Left Vocalist Diana Godfrey (née Raggatt) taking a break at the George, with John, who 'looked after the lights' (c.1955).

Below The Bar at the George was always an exciting place to 'meet up' during a dance, as can be seen by this happy group in May 1951. (By kind permission of the Luton Museum Service).

Cabaret at the George, 1950s style. With support from Geoff Stokes Orchestra, these three ladies are dancing the can-can.

Interval time at 'The George'. Ken Green relaxes with band members, l. to r. Norman Wesley, Derek Impey, Diana Godfrey, Ken and Vince Shepherd (c early 1950s).

At 82, and still playing piano at the Queens Head, Tebworth, the legendary Billy Seaford recalled to me his very colourful career as a 'lounge' bar or dance band pianist which brought him from his home town of Barry, South Wales to Luton. Playing aboard the luxury cruise liners between Bermuda and New York in the 1930s was remembered with affection, as well as his days at the George Hotel with various bands.

Billy was witness to an evening at the Winter Assembly Hall, Luton in 1936, when Louis Armstrong took time off from his show at the London Palladium to "do a

The Bill Seaford Quintet at RAF Stanbridge (c.mid 1960s). L. to r.: Bill Spence (Vocals); John Collier (Drums); Laurie Jeffs (Guitar); Jimmy Stead (Tenor Sax); Bill Seaford (Piano). Bill would have augmented players for this (Christmas?) gig.

gig" with the St. Louis Players, which included local star Reggie Goff in the line-up. (Louis insisted on his fee before he took to the stage though!).

Billy was also a virtuoso on the cinema organ, and for a while was resident organist at the Alma, the same time that famous Doreen Chadwick was resident organist at the Ritz cinema, Gordon Street (c.1948). One of the shows at the Alma Theatre that Billy was associated with was 'Memories of Jolson' and Bill was asked to rehearse a young starlet from the show, who was being groomed for bigger things. It paid off, because that young trooper was Shirley Bassey.

Bill has continuously played in the area for over 60 years, giving so much pleasure to those of us who enjoy our music in the 'relaxed' style, for listening or dancing to. Commissioned in the year 1998 to go to Belgium, he recorded a CD of lounge bar piano music for the American market, a copy of which he gave me when I visited him at his bungalow in Houghton Regis.

IN THE MOOD FOR LOVE

Bill Seaford

I'm In The Mood For Love • Fly Me To The Moon
Satin Doll • Moon River • Shadow Of Your Smile • Misty

Every picture tells a story, 80 years old and still playing! The cover of Bill Seaford's 1998 released CD.

On Tuesday 28th August 2001, I took a casual day's holiday to extend the Bank Holiday break, and entered Littlewoods store from George Street, when the most remarkable coincidence took place. Littlewoods is where the George Hotel used to be, and who should I bump into – non other than John Lambert, who was the baritone sax player in the Ken Green Orchestra, whose shoulder I used to look over when I looked at what they were playing. John was with his wife Ann, who is drummer Freddie Wells' sister, and we all had a most enjoyable chat about old times in the Littlewoods café. John had taken over as baritone in Ken Green's band

SATURDAY
TELEGRAPH HOME EDITION

No. 4958   © Home Counties Newspapers, Ltd., 1965   Postage on this issue is 1d   **Saturday, May 15, 1965**   Lighting-up Time: 9.15 p.m.   Price 3d.

'The George' to become super store

THE George Hotel, Luton, has been sold to Littlewoods Mail Order Stores, Ltd., and is to be demolished to make way for a large department store.

The hotel will close towards the end of next month or the middle of July.

The price paid by Littlewoods has not been disclosed.

Yesterday, Mr. Rex Randall, of Thomas Thorne and Co., chartered auctioneers and estate agents, of King Street, Luton, who has been acting on behalf of the George, declined to comment on reports that it was in the region of £750,000.

THREE SHOPS INVOLVED

The sale has been made subject to existing leases for three shops in George Street which form part of the hotel building.

These are James Walker. Ltd., the jewellers, S. and M. Fashions, and Neville Reed, men's fashions.

In each case, the lease should have some years to run, but the future of the businesses will now be a matter for negotiation between them and the new owners.

The hotel has been owned by the Fisher family for more than 40 years, and is the last of their business interests in Luton.

Mr. Charles Fisher, who for the last five years has represented the family in the company's affairs, said the company had disposed of the property with reluctance.

It is understood that the hotel was not put on the market, but for some time, various approaches had been made from organisations wishing to build stores in the town.

Littlewoods is understood to have come into the picture

quite recently, and the final negotiations were conducted swiftly.

The present hotel building replaced an old coaching inn.

Letters will go out next week to people who have booked the hotel for functions after July.

Left The expected news still came as a bombshell.

Below The 'George' did reopen for a short while, but the Arndale Shopping Precinct was being built, which would ensure only the briefest respite for the dance hall.

Pictorial

No. 5101   Postage on this issue is 5d.   **Tuesday, October 4, 1966**   Weekly net sales 14,006   3d.

A full mixture is wanted at the George

Another shot in the arm was given to Luton's ailing social life with the re-opening of the George Hotel.

Last week nearly 2,000 people attended the opening night of the National Dance Club at the George Street hotel.

The club — open to members only — is attempting to obtain a drinks licence for seven days a week. At the moment, a licence has

been issued for four evenings.

Behind the scheme are four Irishmen, who are

believed to live in Luton. Manager Tom Fletcher said, "I am not sure if they would like me to disclose their names."

Mr. Fletcher, himself an Irishman, emphasised that the club was not intended only for Luton's large Irish population.

"We hope to get all sorts here," he said. "And by making the club for members only we hope to avoid getting a bad reputation," he added.

from Vince Shepherd, and, when the George closed, spent 9 years on lead alto sax with the Tommy Thompson Orchestra, and a few more years with the Bob Bown Combo. They said Tommy Thompson would not allow any smoking or drinking on the stage, but was a very decent and fair bandleader. Ann reminded us that Les Vass was then the manager and M.C. of Tommy's Band and she always waited in anticipation when Les announced the food interval. He always said "buff-it" is served, instead of boofey!!

The Tommy Thompson Orchestra (c.1960) at the staff canteen, Vauxhall Motors, Luton. Line-up: rhythm section: Terry Exley (Piano); Lou Ferraro (Bass); Dally Hughes (Drums); front line l. to r.: Jimmy Marsh (Trumpet); Harold Stott (2nd Alto Sax); Alan Whittle (lead Alto); Tommy Thompson (lead Tenor Sax); Stan Tisbury (2nd Tenor).

M.C. for the evening, Les Vass, shows off a raffle prize to a bevy of young ladies at the Christ Church Old Boys Dance at the George Hotel on 1st May 1951. (By kind permission of the Luton Museum Service)

The Scene

Although the social scene began to change dramatically in the 1960s as the public Dance Halls were all closing, there were still a great many private functions offering live music and entertainment throughout the week.

The Halfway House (now a Beefeater), Dunstable, was a Public House with extensive facilities for Dinner/Dances, Concerts or just Dances. Their own Sunday evening concerts were hugely popular, where they booked top show bands, who shared the evening with local bands. We played there on many Sundays as the 'house' band. For about 20 years it has to be said that the Halfway House was the most popular of the local venues available for privately booked Dinner/Dances, the busiest evenings being Friday and Saturday. Bernard Hemmings had been moved to the Halfway House from the Glen Eagle Hotel, Harpenden (same proprietors), where he was now functions/catering manager, and was as much a part of the function as the building itself. I used to watch him from the piano, and the waitresses would not move until he brushed his hair, or similar, then, as one, they would commence serving or collecting. His trademark was a green carnation which would be freshly delivered for each function.

LAPORTE INDUSTRIES LIMITED
GENERAL CHEMICALS DIVISION

LAPORTE

LAPORTE TWENTYFIVE YEAR CLUB

ANNUAL DINNER

1970

Halfway House Hotel, Dunstable

Chairman .... The Rt. Hon. Lord Hill of Luton

Tuesday, 13th October,
7 - 30 p.m.

Piano only for this one – during dinner. The Guest of Honour being the Rt. Hon Lord Hill of Luton, or as I remember him for his wartime medical advice 'The Radio Doctor'. Charles Hill was Luton's M.P. in the 1950s and Chancellor of the Duchy of Lancaster.

'The Chiltern Trio', in the Chiltern Room, at the Halfway House, Dunstable. Alan Higgs (Drums); Lloyd Connet (Double Bass); Bill Seaford (Piano).

Tommy Thompson and Basil Osman were stalwarts of the Musicians Union for many years, and, to their credit, their bands voluntarily played at many charitable and fundraising functions. That's not to say that I wasn't involved with the M.U., because I was also a prominent committee man, helping run the successful Monday evening M.U. socials.

Through the late 1960s into the 1970s and 80s, guest bands, newly formed outfits or rehearsal bands gave their services:

To help raise money for the union.

To give bands valuable exposure to the public.

To use the evening as a good 'public relations' exercise for the union.

To allow musicians the opportunity to socialise together and to take out their wives and girlfriends, because at weekends they would be otherwise occupied.

The home base for the socials was the Hatters Club at the football ground Kenilworth Road, Luton, but occasionally they would be organised out of town, to cover the area of the membership catchment. In the very early days, the socials were held at the Biscot Mill, Luton, but it soon became restricted for space as their popularity increased, so we (the union) had to move to the Hatters.

Tommy Thompson with his 'house band', at the Musicians' Ball in the Cresta, October 1956. This was a familiar role for Tommy, on tenor sax, who on this occasion was joined by Tom Stark (Piano), Harold Ward (Bass) and Pete 'Rhythm is our business' Green (Drums).

Tommy and Amy Thompson surrounded by friends at their 25th wedding anniversary celebrations at the Biscot Mill, Luton, on November 12th 1969. From l. to r. (unfortunately some guests unknown): Reg Clark (M.C.) holding mic.; Barry Imber (Piano); Dave Cunningham (Vocals); Tommy (Violin) & Amy; Basil Osman (holding drumsticks); Kenny Gorrell (Drums) sitting; Jim Marsh (Trumpet); John Lambert (Sax); Harry Hussey (Accordion).

Right The Nat Coleman quartet at the Hatters Club early 1970s, with Tricia Howard on vocals. The band: Ron Franks (Organ); Drummer (unknown); Denny Cox (Bass Guitar/Leader).

The Vauxhall Dixieland Band guesting at a 1960s Musicians Union Ball at the Civic Centre, Dunstable. Line-up l. to r.: Jack Tattersall (Double Bass); Ron Hull (Piano); John Murray (Clarinet/Alto Sax); Don Barrett (Tenor Sax); Denis Hyde (Trumpet); Cliff Royal (Trombone); Freddie Wells (Drums) almost hidden, centre. Incidentally, Cliff Royal was another local brass player who doubled on cello.

Midweek dances were keeping us even busier, at the ever popular Hatters Club at Luton Town F.C.

Mention the musicians' social evenings, and who could forget Dorothy 'Dot' Brown and husband Dennis who could be relied upon to run the door, the raffles, and be on hand generally to marshal the evening. Dot was a super pianist and, together with Dennis, travelled throughout Beds and Herts at weekends to play at the many venues always after her services – latterly on organ.

1966 saw the opening of Cesar's Palace Night-club on the site of the old Luton dog track on Skimpot Road. It was just like Las Vegas coming to Luton, with dancing girls, top international cabaret, gaming tables and the Geoff Walker Band supplying the music for dancing and support for the cabaret. I was fortunate enough to be present on the opening night, when Tommy Cooper supplied the cabaret and, later on, two of my favourite recording stars Lena Martell and Frankie Laine had bookings there. I didn't see them, but Tom Jones (Oct.1967) and Dickie Valentine (Feb.1968) sang there to packed houses. Dickie Valentine's recording of 'Finger of Suspicion' was the first record Mum had bought to play on our new GEC radiogram (in 1954) with its 'diamond stylus' needle. Up to then record players had replaceable steel throwaway (or re-sharpen) needles.

Through the 1960s, 70s and 80s private functions were well supported either as social functions or for fund raising. Departments and organisations would use them as 'get-togethers' and arrange such functions as 'Pie'n Peas Dance', 'Sausage and Mash Do', 'Fish and Chip Supper', or a multitude of other functions such as fancy dress dances or Cheese and Wine social evenings. All needed live groups or bands, and we were out there taking our share of the spoils.

The Starlights were one of the most popular groups in town, supplying the latest music to both dance and club circuit. This 1970 shot shows l. to r.: Arthur Tuck (Organ); Bette Lee (Vocals); Gilson Lavis (Drums); John Stares (Bass Guitar). Luton-born Gilson Lavis is now drummer for the radio & TV recording star Jools Holland, and Sunderland-born Bette was a hugely popular vocalist, booked by many of the area's top dance bands, including Geoff Stokes and Johnny (Harding) & The Rainbows.

Musicians Union   (Luton Branch)

PRESENT A

SAUSAGE & MASH BUFFET DANCE

at The Vauxhall Motors
AL CANTEEN 'RED' Dining Room
Osborne Road, Luton

on Friday, 10th September, 1982
8-00 p.m. to 12-00 Midnight

DANCING TO LIVE MUSIC

Spot Prizes   Raffle   Ticket £2-00

Rights of Admission Reserved

LUTON TOWN BOWLING CLUB
TENNIS SECTION

ANNUAL   DANCE

FRIDAY, DECEMBER 4th

DANCING TO THE

Ray Miller Band

Bar Extension   · 8 p.m. to 1 a.m.
Dark lounge suit
or evening dress   1 GUINEA

Above left Privately-organised functions were commonplace, and well supported, for fundraising and social get-togethers. The 'Blue' and 'Red' rooms at the Vauxhall Brache Centre, were popular venues, and hired out at most weekends.
Above right 1970 – One Guinea admission to this dance, at their clubhouse in Bowling Green Lane, Old Bedford Road.

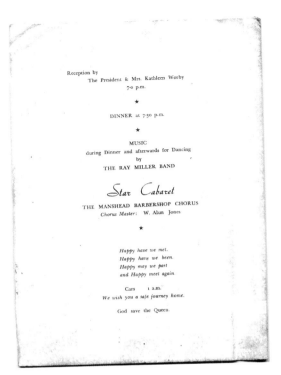

LOVELLS BURY LODGE 4018

Ladies' Festival

FRIDAY, 5th MAY, 1978.

President W.Bro. L. C. WORBY

The Worshipful Master, Officers and Brethren of The Lovells Bury Lodge welcome you to their Ladies' Festival and sincerely hope that you will have a really enjoyable evening with us all.

Reception by
The President & Mrs. Kathleen Worby
7·0 p.m.

★

DINNER at 7·30 p.m.

★

MUSIC
during Dinner and afterwards for Dancing
by
THE RAY MILLER BAND

Star Cabaret

THE MANSHEAD BARBERSHOP CHORUS
Chorus Master: W. Alun Jones

★

Happy have we met.
Happy have we been.
Happy may we part
and Happy meet again.

Cars 1 a.m.
We wish you a safe journey home.

God save the Queen.

1978 – Cars at 1.00am from the Halfway House. Star cabaret at this one!

At these functions, a cabaret act would often be booked for the interval, and although they were probably very good, and often very famous, they invariably needed backing with music, which was a continual source of aggravation with most musicians, because (a) they were due to perform when the band was set for a break; (b) they expected the band to play without any prior rehearsal, and (c) bandsmen should be paid extra for the accompaniment of a cabaret, but often no allowance was made for this payment. If a cabaret was booked with complete disregard to these facts, total acrimony was guaranteed, as we could vouch on many occasions.

Discos were by now able to supply a full evening's music for dancing, and were as popular as live bands, and were becoming at many functions the only music booked. This wouldn't have suited the older clientele, so many functions (dinner dances especially) ran 50/50 music, that was half live music, and half disco. The Musicians Union was working hard nationally to maintain the employment of live musicians. I had mixed feelings on these nights, but at least we had plenty of breaks.

A well organised function always had an M.C. (Master of Ceremonies) for use during the dinner, and then often continued on during the dancing, although most bands preferred to do their own announcing, etc. The busiest and most popular M.C. and Toastmaster was Reg Clark, whose sense of humour, experience and true professionalism would guarantee the smooth running of whatever function he was booked for. He never 'got in the hair' of the band and had a good working relationship with all musicians.

Rotary Club of Leighton Buzzard
President: J. G. DELAFIELD

Ladies' Night
to be held at
THE HALFWAY HOUSE, LUTON
FRIDAY, 12th MAY, 1978
7.30 for 8.00 p.m. until 1.00 a.m.

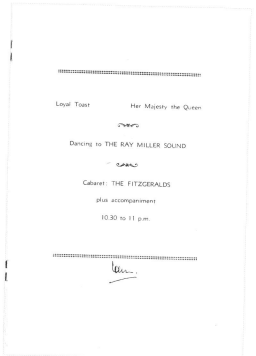

Loyal Toast   Her Majesty the Queen

Dancing to THE RAY MILLER SOUND

Cabaret: THE FITZGERALDS

plus accompaniment

10.30 to 11 p.m.

1978 – Another cabaret at the Halfway House.

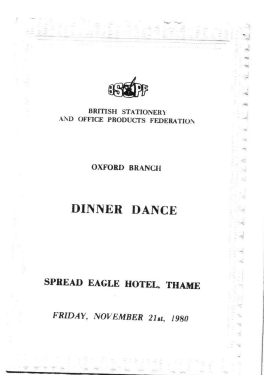

BRITISH STATIONERY
AND OFFICE PRODUCTS FEDERATION

OXFORD BRANCH

DINNER DANCE

SPREAD EAGLE HOTEL, THAME

FRIDAY, NOVEMBER 21st, 1980

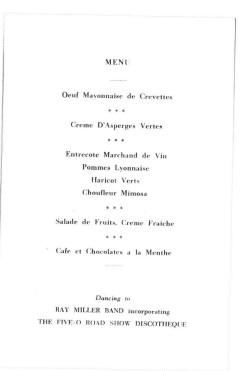

MENU

Oeuf Mayonnaise de Crevettes

* * *

Creme D'Asperges Vertes

* * *

Entrecote Marchand de Vin
Pommes Lyonnaise
Haricot Verts
Choufleur Mimosa

* * *

Salade de Fruits, Creme Fraiche

* * *

Cafe et Chocolates a la Menthe

Dancing to
RAY MILLER BAND incorporating
THE FIVE-O ROAD SHOW DISCOTHEQUE

To cater for all age groups, many functions would book a discotheque to share the evening with a live band.

A bag full of 'spot prizes' was often supplied for the band leader to distribute during the evening, to keep the dancers on their toes. Questions such as "The first person to reach me with black teeth" (a comb), "A picture of Queen Victoria" (a coin) or "A pair of nickers" (2 × £1 notes) etc. etc. would win themselves and partner, a prize. I used to ask my own spot prize questions, which were taken from words of a song, such as:

Who was fined $50 for drinking water?

(The first to shout out)

A politicians daughter! (was the winner).

Song. The Coffee Song

"A politicians daughter

Was accused of drinking water

And was fined a great big $50 bill

Cause there's an awful lot of coffee in Brazil!".

I would vary the questions asked by using many different songs as above.

Dances such as the Paul Jones, intended to mix up the crowd, or the Palais Glide, were casualties of the era, never to return to the dance floor.

Paul Jones: Men form a circle, hands held, Ladies form a circle inside the men's – also hands held.

Music starts, to tunes such as "Here we go round the Mulberry Bush" and circles revolve in opposite directions.

Music stops, and who ever you are facing – you dance the next dance with.

Palais Glide: All dancers linked in lines, with arms around shoulders and move round the floor 'in waves' to numbers such as "Horsey, Horsey" and "All by Yourself in the Moonlight".

Throughout the time covered by these recollections, the Musicians Union was a dominant feature of the scene. It was almost compulsory to be a member, and otherwise it severely restricted the venues you could play at and the musicians you could book. The union did work hard for its members, and the Chairman – for as long as I can remember – was Tommy Thompson. Tommy saw out a few Secretaries, and those I remember were: Ray Sills; Philip 'Pip' Hallman; Derek Impey; Barry Imber; Basil Osman; Jimmy Stead and Ron Franks.

Tommy ran his own orchestra and also a very successful entertainment agency. His wife Amy was also totally committed to their enterprises whether in their shop (The Luton Music Centre, 114 Leagrave Road) the orchestra, the union or the agency. Lutonian Tommy (b.1925) was primarily tenor sax, but occasionally showed his prowess on violin, Stephan Grappelli style, and Amy, who hailed from Middlesborough, was a most competent pianist, and gave piano lessons. They jointly retired and moved to Wisbech in 1991. Their son Lindsey was a proficient drummer and bass guitarist.

During the heyday of the dance bands, musicians were well provided for by three excellent music shops. They were S.Farmer & Co, whose 'L' shape shop fronted 83 George Street, round to 2 Wellington Street; Arthur Day & Sons, 15/17

At the George Hotel, Young Liberal Conservatives take to the floor for the Palais Glide at their dance on 7th April 1951. (By kind permission of the Luton Museum Service)

Close up of above. (By kind permission of the Luton Museum Service)

Upper George Street; and Bone & Co, who were musical instrument dealers and repairers at 7 New Bedford Road. A retail business still operates from the premises, and some of the original ceramic tiles, depicting musical instruments, are still visible on the outside of the shop. Unfortunately they became casualties of the declining music scene, which left Luton depleted of specialist music shops, until Tommy Thompson opened his shop in Leagrave Road.

Getting together! An early 1960s session at the Leicester Arms, featuring l. to r.: Freddie Wells; Bruce Bonfield; Melvin Colebrook; Billy Lee (Trumpet); Tom Stark (Piano).

Hazel's Fish and Chip shop in Leagrave Road, on the corner of Fitzroy Avenue, always stayed open at weekends until late, and many a bandsman used to stop off on the way home to buy their supper. From the mid 1960s and through the 1970s I would often buy fish and chips to take home, where Margaret and I would eat them watching a 'B' movie, and take the opportunity to generally unwind. How the 'gigs' went was relived at Hazel's, which in its own way became quite a focal point for gossip and a contact point for many local musicians. It became commonplace to see men in dress suits and bow ties, eating their Fish and Chips outside Hazel's until the early hours.

There were drawbacks at having to wear a bow tie and dress suit, as standard band apparel, especially if a 'gig' was used as an excuse to have a cheeky night out. Many a musician was spotted in a quiet pub on a Monday or Tuesday with his bow tie on, and a music case by his side!

Through the early 1970s Margaret and I always tried to get out one night a week and that always tended to be Thursdays. Margaret's Mum Edie generally baby-sat, and, even if we went to a country pub first, we invariably finished up in the Lounge Bar at the Royal Hotel, Mill Street, where there was always a band playing, our favourite being Steve Mason and his Dixieland Band. It had a great atmosphere, and remained a popular music bar until its closure as a public house. Steve's popularity was such that he released an LP called 'It Don't Mean A Thing If It Ain't Got That Swing' after one of his best numbers.

Above Dunstable-born trumpeter Norman Willison fronting his own band at the Leicester Arms, early 1950s, supported by Ron Franks (Piano), Derek Tearle (Drums), Dick Tomlinson (Double Bass) and Derek Wheldon (Tenor Sax).

Left The Nat Coleman Band taking a break at the Royal Hotel, Mill Street, Luton (early 1970s). Line-up, top to bottom: Roy Evans (Drums); Ron Franks (Keyboard); Bette Lee (Vocals); Dennis Cox (Bass Guitar). For a while, Dennis teamed up with accordionist Harry Hussey and drummer George Meyer to be part of the Winston Trio.

Steve Mason & his Dixieland Band at the Royal Hotel, Mill Street, Luton (late 1960s).
Personnel l. to r.: Bob Bates (Trombone); Peter Green (Drums); Steve Mason (Trumpet);
Denny Cox (Bass Guitar); Roy Grundy (Alto Sax, Tenor Sax, Clarinet); Keith Rolt (Piano).

Ray Scarbrow was the landlord of The Somerset Tavern from Oct 1965 to Feb 1983 and was always keen to promote live music at every opportunity. Mondays at the Tavern became an institution, where jazz musicians and followers would pack into the lounge bar to let their hair down. From our band, Jimmy (tenor sax and flute) and Kenny (drums) were regulars, and augmented with other musicians who enjoyed playing jazz to provide music of the very highest standard without prior rehearsal.

Opposite above Steve Mason & his Dixieland Band at the Royal, line-up: Roy Grundy (Saxes & Clarinet); Kenny Keats (Trombone); Steve Mason (Trumpet/Vocals); Keith Rolt (Piano); Arthur Indge (Guitar/Banjo); Brian Grieves (Bass); Peter Green (Drums/Vocals).

Opposite below An impromptu jazz session, this time at the Leicester Arms, Dunstable Rd, Luton (late 1950s). George Ashby (Trombone); Keith Burgoine (Drums); Vernon Critten – junior (Double Bass); Norman Willison (Trumpet); Bill Harris (Piano); Geoff Stokes (Alto Sax).

The Wayfarers, a very busy and popular Dunstable-based band, and, in great demand for dance and Dixieland functions, are shown here playing at the Lea Manor Sports centre in the early 1980s. Line-up l. to r.: Jim Collins (Trombone); Graham Scriven (Drums); Brian Jones (Trumpet); Alan Small (Bass Guitar); Tony Ward (Clarinet/Sax). On piano is Mick Stone, behind Tony on clarinet. Prior to Alan joining the band, Trevor Evans was their bass player for many years, whom I used as a dep. on quite a few occasions.

The Wayfarers also played there often, as we did, but generally speaking the 'ensemble' would comprise individuals joining up for a musicians' night out, with perhaps the occasional 'star' being pre booked for a special attraction. The Wayfarers, one of the oldest and most popular of bands, were formed in Dunstable in 1957, and were as much in demand for either conventional dancing or Dixieland jazz.

Other regulars were Wally Bramhall (tenor sax); Phil Brown (clarinet); Harry Hussey (accordion); Roger Parker (piano); Bob Usher (bass guitar); Stuart Horn (piano); George Meyer and Freddie Wells (drums); Geoff Vickers (trumpet); bass guitarist Ron Adams, and many more; (together with drummer Graham Scriven, Ron Adams presented a jazz programme on Radio Bedfordshire – later to become Three Counties Radio – for 10 years from 1985). Professional Al Gaye, who was a member of the Alex Welsh Band, was a superb tenor saxophonist, and was one of the 'stars' who guested at The Somerset.

When Ray vacated the tenancy of the Tavern, the new manager, Alan Mayes (who had been managing the Halfway House until then) was an excellent

The Wayfarers at a 1960s formal function at Rothamsted Park, Harpenden. Line-up: back row l. to r.: Mike Parker (Bass); Cliff Knott (Guitar); Mick Stone (Piano); George Wallace (Drums); front row l. to r.: Tony Ward (Clarinet); Brian Jones (Trumpet); Jim Collins (Trombone).

trumpeter, and not only continued with the Monday night jazz evenings, but played himself, until its gradual demise shortly afterwards. Alan's brother 'Chic', also a trumpeter, was very popular and famous in Scotland.

The most renowned of the local hostelries where regular and impromptu jazz sessions took place, allowing local jazz musicians to rub shoulders with famous 'guests', were undoubtedly the Angel Inn at Toddington and the Cross Keys at Pulloxhill.

By the late 1970s there were not too many big semi-pro bands still running, but Eddie Curtis (Princes Risborough) was one of the exceptions, and was still in great demand. I heard a recording of theirs at Oxford Town Hall on New Years Eve 1980, and it featured Lutonian Jimmy Marsh (2nd trumpet) playing the legendary trumpet solo 'I can't get started'. He wouldn't have played better, at any time in his career. Great stuff. (The 2nd trumpeter in a band's line up, was usually the one who took the solos).

**Members of the Chris Rogers band at a function at Wrest Park, Silsoe (early 1970s).
L. to r.: Jim Marsh (Trumpet); Alan Collier (Piano); Bette Lee (Vocals); Brian Arnall
(Leader/Tenor Sax); John Lambert (Alto Sax).**

In general, pianos in the halls were not being kept up to par, with notes not playing, pedals not working and as often as not they were out of tune. There were exceptions of course, such as council halls and schools, but even there the pianos were often locked away or not on the stage at week-ends. This prompted a lot of pianists to switch to (a portable) organ, especially as they were becoming the featured instrument on a growing number of chart hits, the most popular being Procol Harum's 1972 hit 'A Whiter Shade of Pale'. Drummer Ray Dennis read the trend, switching to organ at just the right time, and became very popular for quite a while. He was in great demand, not only because of the instrument, as he was a natural, with a beautiful style. Years earlier to give the piano a bit of 'added dimension', some pianists added a clavioline to the piano, which was a single electronic keyboard, designed to give the smaller outfit more variation to their sound, but it had limited appeal.

Most bands enjoyed playing at the Queensway Hall, Dunstable. Here on organ is Norman Wesley with Melvin Colebrook (Accordion) and Alec Sims (Drums).

The Jimmy Harrison Trio (c.1960s). Jim Thompson (Drums); Percy Jeffs (Bass); Jimmy Harrison (Piano). Note Percy using a bow on the bass, and clavioline fixed to piano keyboard.

15-year-old Diane Hutchins playing 'The Christie' at Stotfold Working Mens Club on November 19th 1974.

The old Regent cinema at Stotfold was converted into a Working Men's Club, and, to their credit, the cinema's Christie organ was left intact as part of the club's entertainment attractions. The stage was huge, and the workings of the organ took up the whole of the area beneath the stage, which vibrated when the organ was warming up. Many different organists alternated to entertain the patrons, and some of them were so keen, they played before the evening had started, as well as during the interval. One of them, Diane Hutchins from Luton, was emerging as a very talented, and attractive, exponent of the organ, and for someone so young had the confidence and poise of an old hand. She was gaining valuable experience as a soloist, and soon became established on the club scene with her duo or trio. The dedication received from her totally supportive parents Les and Madge certainly paid dividends. Coincidentally, when she married Nick Brown, she became another D. Brown on the circuit, joining Dot Brown (no relation) who had been a prominent pianist/organist for many years.

Sports days with an evening dance were held annually by Vauxhall Motors, Laportes and Electrolux and would usually have a celebrity guest as the central attraction. One year the Electrolux booked Frankie Vaughan (c. late 1950s) who was at the height of his popularity, and attracted a large crowd during the day and at the evening's dance. Singing star Frankie was always immaculately turned out with evening suit and bow tie and always wore a Luton made boater during his act, manipulated to great advantage, to give each number he delivered the necessary panache.

Vauxhall Motors Recreation Club LUTON SOCIAL SECTION *presents*

Special Non-Stop Modern Carnival

DANCE

(In Conjunction with Annual Sports Spectacular Day)

MAIN DINING HALL

SAT., 8th JUNE, 1963

7.30 p.m. to Midnight   Doors Open 7.15 p.m.

Non-stop dancing to the music of YOUR FAVOURITE DANCE BANDS

KEN GREEN	SUPPORTED BY	RAY MILLER
and His 10 Piece	*Luton's Premier Rock Group*	and His 10 Piece Band
ORCHESTRA	Tony Stevens	
	and	*Featuring*
Featuring	THE QUINTONES	London Stars and Lady Vocalist
Lady Vocalist		

Tickets can be obtained from your
AREA COMMITTEE MEMBERS

TICKETS 6/- EACH

NO TICKETS WILL BE SOLD AT THE DOOR

ALSO FROM
CANTEEN SHOPS — LUTON & DUNSTABLE
RECREATION OFFICE — LUTON
RECREATION OFFICE — DUNSTABLE

Admission at the Bar for visitors is by Membership Card only. Temporary Membership Cards can be obtained on application by a Member to the Recreation Office etc.

THURSDAY 6th JUNE, 1963

WILL CLUB MEMBERS PLEASE NOTE THAT THEY MUST PRODUCE THEIR WORKS PASS BEFORE ADMITTANCE TO THE BAR AND NO EXCEPTION WILL BE MADE TO THIS RULE.

Rights of Admission Reserved

TWO BARS	Balloons Streamers	Light Refreshments served in
Management Group Dining Room		Staff Dining Room only
and Canteen Bar	Spot Prizes	Separate Tables

Admittance by Main Entrance to Canteen (opposite visitors car park)   Use of visitors car park

Cloakroom inside Main Canteen — Fee 3d.

COME ALONG AND BRING ALL YOUR FRIENDS

We climbed the ladder and reached the top. Sharing top billing with Ken Green and his Orchestra at the 1963 Vauxhall Sports Day Dance, not forgetting Tony Stevens & the Quintones Rock Group of course.

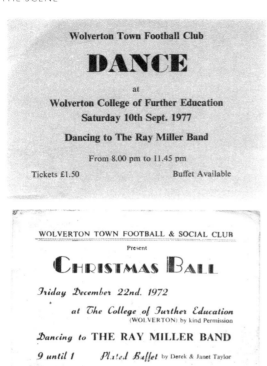

Wolverton Town Football Club

DANCE

at

**Wolverton College of Further Education
Saturday 10th Sept. 1977**

Dancing to The Ray Miller Band

From 8.00 pm to 11.45 pm

Tickets £1.50   Buffet Available

WOLVERTON TOWN FOOTBALL & SOCIAL CLUB

Present

CHRISTMAS BALL

Friday December 22nd. 1972

at *The College of Further Education*
(WOLVERTON) by kind Permission

Dancing to **THE RAY MILLER BAND**

9 until 1   *Plated Buffet* by Derek & Janet Taylor

Tickets £1.50   *Dress Optional*

Above 1972 & 1977 – Keeping in with
Wolverton F.C. *Below* 1979 – Tally Ho!

Oakley Hunt Branch of the Pony Club

JUNIOR HUNT BALL

at Addison Centre, Kempston
on Thursday, January 11th 1979

7.30 p.m. for 8.00 p.m. till 1.00 a.m.

Dancing to The Ray Miller Band.

Dinner 7.30 p.m. for 8.00 p.m.   4 course Hot Meal
Licenced Bar   Evening dress or Dark Lounge Suit
Ticket £4

The small railway town of Wolverton and its neighbouring towns of Stony Stratford and New Bradwell (now part of Milton Keynes) produced some excellent semi-professional dance bands from the 1940s through to the 80s, all performing over a wide area, including Luton, the foremost being the Rhythm Aces, led by Doug Dytham and the Tommy Clarridge Big Band. From the Rhythm Aces, the Roland Anstruther Combo was formed, led by Dennis Smith (alto sax & vocals) and included Don Payne (trumpet) and Nicky Dytham (Doug's son) on bass.

I became great friends with the Combo, and not only did we "pass on" work to each other, but they often played at our Musicians Union social evenings at the Hatters Club.

The other neighbouring area of Mid Herts was also closely entwined with Luton, and many long term friendships between bandleaders and musicians were created. Although evidence of these strong links are highlighted throughout the book, meeting bass player Dennis 'Denny' Cox in February 2003 resulted in some additional snippets of interest.

Opposite above Dennis Cox came out of the RAF in 1954 and formed the Nat Coleman Band, which he led on electric guitar. Shown here in 1955/6, Denny is supported by: Mike Holmes (Drums); Brian Kinsey (Double Bass); Ken Gurrelli (Piano). Already on electric guitar, Denny soon switched to playing the electric 'bass' guitar because of the demand, due to the shortage of experienced players.

Opposite below Based at Welwyn Garden City, George Thorby ran an excellent big band for many years. Here George is fronting the band (c.1960s), and on sax, next to trumpeter, is Brian Benton who is still very active in the promotion of live music.

Denny was already an accomplished electric guitar player in Watford before he moved to Luton in 1962, and played regularly with Alex Miller at the Water End Barn (St. Albans), The Spot (London Colney) and the Comet (Hatfield). As well as playing for a host of other bands, he also ran his own dance band, which he called the Nat Coleman Band and became Luton's first osteopath when he opened his business in Dunstable Road in 1979.

Bands from Luton often guested at Mid Herts musicians' union functions, and vice versa.

Left Denny in the more familiar stance with bass guitar.

One of the busiest and most popular groups in town was the Ajax Trio, with Lutonian Bob Peters on organ, Mick McGuinness (Tenor Sax) and Eric Monk (Drums) shown here mid 1960s.

The Ray Miller Quintet

We were entering the mid 1960s as a 5 piece, and although we took work for anything from Trio to Sextet the quintet was ideal both for sound and management. Derek on lead guitar/vocals was a superb exponent, and together with Tony on rhythm guitar could be relied upon to "more than pull their weight" when required. As a trio, Derek, Tony and Jerry knitted perfectly to produce background music of the highest calibre for restaurants or

The Ray Miller Quintet – versatile and busy. 1.Stuart Goodyear. 2.Jimmy Stead. 3.Jerry Blain. 4.Tony Reynolds. 5.Bob Bates.

dinner dances, and with many venues not having a piano their versatility was invaluable. Derek was a one off, was game for anything, and above all always cheerful.

As young marrieds, we all had problems occasionally with transport and on more than one occasion Derek (as a lorry driver at that time) volunteered to pick me and Jerry (drums) up in his lorry. Minus his lorry, he then bought a Cadillac and often used it to transport the band. The car was something else, and caused quite a stir wherever we went. Derek was quick to introduce the latest songs, with 'Bachelor Boy' and 'Av You Got a Light Boy' being two of the most popular, but he always enjoyed singing a selection of Bobby Darin's numbers. Finally, though, Derek's wife Rose gave birth to Tina their second child and he decided to call it a day.

As Tony and Derek were very close, and had joined the band together, I was concerned that Tony would leave also, but that was not to be the case. Tony came south from Liverpool with his wife Thelma in 1957 to work for English Electric at Luton Airport, which later merged into British Aerospace at Stevenage. He lived in Denbigh Road, Luton before moving with his family to Stevenage in 1963. He often related stories of his youth when he was in the Merchant Navy and how he learnt to play the guitar. On one particular ship there was no individual who could accompany their 'sing songs', so one of the crew asked Tony if he played guitar, to which young Tony said "No". "Well you do now", was the answer, and he was handed an old guitar, and had no option but to learn – quick. He never had any lessons, but had a remarkable aptitude for picking up any song, in any key! To his credit, and although he travelled from Stevenage, Tony became not only a linch-pin in the band, but a great friend for almost 20 years. I was most saddened when Tony died in 1997.

It was necessary to replace Derek with a versatile front man, and, whether it was luck or inspiration, Jimmy Stead was contacted and fortunately was able to take on the commitment to be our lead instrument on tenor sax. In return, I was able to offer the band 2/3 engagements every week, which was an obvious incentive to attract the best musicians. During our very first gig, not only did Jim slot in beautifully, but we found out that he also sang and played flute! Jimmy, who had started playing semi-pro music on his tenor as a 10 year old around Ossett, Dewsbury & Wakefield, left his home (in Ossett) at 17 years of age to join the John Barry Seven in London, who became a household name on the pop scene with many chart hits and regular spots on T.V.'s Drumbeat. The band also did a season at Blackpool with Adam Faith and Emile Ford. He left the band in 1962 and 'did the boats' with trips to Canada and Australia, then came to Luton with wife Rita, who opened a Hairdressing Salon in Biscot Road. John Barry (born John Barry Prendergast) hailed from York, and was destined to become a legendary film composer.

Right Another promotional picture of the John Barry Seven, with Jimmy Stead sitting on the extreme left. The band continued in name, but without the presence of John Barry himself (c.1960). (By kind permission of Harry Hammond archives, V & A picture library)

Above What a bonus for the town, when ex John Barry Seven member Jimmy Stead made
Luton his home. Here, Jimmy, extreme left, on baritone sax, is featured in a publicity
picture for the pop programme 'Drumbeat', with John Barry on trumpet (late 1950s).
(By kind permission of Harry Hammond archives, V& A picture library)

April 1976 at an RAF Wittering, near Peterborough, function. Part of the hall (shown behind us) was bedecked in white camouflage 'snow' netting. Back row: Tony Reynolds (Rhythm Guitar); Bob Bates (Trombone); Jim Stead (Tenor Sax/Flute); kneeling: Kenny Gorrell (Drums); Stuart Goodyear (M.C./Piano). This was our busiest period, and very settled as a 5-piece. Bob, Jim and myself would also vocalise many numbers.

The dye was cast, as with Tony (rhythm guitar), Jerry (drums), Jimmy (Multi talent) and myself on keyboard, vocals and M.C. we would be versatile enough for most engagements and ideally suited to augment if required. Jerry's experience was immediately evident and his knowledge of dance tempos was a real bonus, so much so, he could be relied upon to 'bring us in' if required. The world was our oyster.

We would be picking up some very prestigious dinner/dance bookings at some of the larger local venues such as the Queensway Hall, Dunstable; SKF Canteen, Sundon Park; Vauxhall (Luton) Staff Canteen and many out of town dates like Kodak, Hemel Hempstead; RAF Wittering and RAF Cranwell etc. etc., but, to do the engagements justice, it was felt that an extra player would not only look better, but would also ease the burden on each of us and give employment to another musician. So, another versatile front line man it had to be, and, because of his existing friendship with us, Bob Bates was the man who was approached, and suddenly we were 5 again. Bob had been a member of the Art Childs Jazz Band and the Leaside Seven, on trombone and vocals, and soon slotted in with our segue style of playing. He was regarded as a seasoned professional locally, and his presence in our line-up was to be a real asset, as both he and Jimmy could read or busk, and adapt to spontaneity as required. The Art Childs Jazz Band was the first Trad jazz band in Luton and was formed by apprentices at Vauxhall Motors Limited in 1957. The Leaside Seven were formed later, and rehearsed in the front room at Bob's house at 167 Ashburnham Road – where the piano was!

KODAK LIMITED

A

Long Service
Dinner

for employees of Kodak Limited
who have completed
25 years, 40 years or 50 years
service during 1980

KODAK HOUSE
HEMEL HEMPSTEAD

31st October, 1980

Above The 'Famous Five' – as I shall always remember them – at Kodak's long service presentation dinner/dance 31st October 1980, at Kodak House, Hemel Hempstead. L. to r.: Yours truly (Piano); Jimmy Stead (Sax/Flute); Bob Bates (Trombone); Kenny Gorrell (Drums); Tony Reynolds (Rhythm Guitar). *Left* The programme for the Kodak's long service dinner dance.

Again at Kodak's – in full voice!

Bob, up to this point, had been better known on the Trad. jazz scene, and had also played for recording star Cy Laurie and his Jazzmen, and was offered a full time position, which was declined, through his dad's insistence! Bob injected many of 'his' numbers into our programme and his rendering of 'Proud Mary' and 'Watermelon Man' never failed to lift the crowd. At 61, Bob still plays Dixieland jazz, but has switched from trombone to sousaphone. That band stayed together for nearly 20 years, and was to become the most dominant and memorable part of my time on the local music scene. Our contacts were snowballing with every engagement, and we were able to pick and choose from the high class private function bookings, which were coming in a year in advance.

The Arcade Saddlery
presents a
Buffet Dance
at the
Sun Hotel, Sun Street, Hitchin
on Thursday, February 10th 1972
8 p.m till 1 a.m.

Fashion Show   Cabaret
Dress Optional   Tickets £2.00 each

1972 – At the Sun Hotel, Hitchin, with fashion show and cabaret.

Although experience had taught us to be wary of cabaret acts, we were nonetheless booked continually to accompany them, because we could! Some of the most notable were Frank Carson (Comedian), Ballroom Dance Champions Bob Burgess & Doreen Freeman, Comedy Dance Act Brothers Lees, and the United Kingdom and English Ballroom Champions Michael & Vicky Barr.

However agreeable we were to support cabaret acts, one evening at Dunstable Rugby Club was one to forget. A female vocalist gave us her 'dots' (colloquial for sheet music) just before she was due on, which were hand written manuscript originals. We could not read them and, without the opportunity to run through them with her, she cut her act short after an embarrassing first number. Lessons learned all round!

A young Robert Wolfe came to some of our dances with his parents and during the break entertained on the organ. Robert became, and still is, a top organist and eventually took over as resident at Blackpool Tower.

LUTON ANGLING CLUB
ANNUAL BUFFET DANCE
AND PRIZE PRESENTATION
BARNFIELD COLLEGE REFECTORY
NEW BEDFORD ROAD, LUTON

SATURDAY, 14th MAY, 1977
7.30 until 11.45 p.m.

DANCING TO THE RAY MILLER BAND

ADMISSION BY TICKET ONLY ... ... £1.75 (£1 Juniors)
Knife and Fork Cold Buffet   Licensed Bar
Lucky Ticket Prize

1977 – At Barnfield College, for Luton Angling Club.

Always on the look-out for top class instrumentalists, who could either do cabaret spots which we were often asked to provide, or sit in with the band to cover for holidays/sickness etc., brought me in touch with Jules Ruben from Hendon who was the most brilliant pianist and organist. He did a great many cabaret turns with us and was often asked to do repeat engagements. His speciality

The Bedfordshire Lodge of St. John the Baptist No. 475

President: W.Bro. E. P. KIRBY

Ladies' Festival

at The Queensway Hall, Dunstable
on Friday, 24th February 1978

Dinner Music
by
THE RAY MILLER TRIO

—

Dancing
to
THE RAY MILLER BAND

—

Cabaret
featuring
MICHAEL & VICKY BARR
The Reigning English Professional Ballroom Champions
and
United Kingdom Professional Ten dance Champions

—

FESTIVAL COMMITTEE

W.BRO. H. E. J. McGEORGE (Sec)   W.BRO. E. KING
W.BRO. E. S. EGAN   W.BRO. J. WHITHAM
W.BRO. P. D. CONGREVE   W BRO. E. KIRBY
BRO. K. BISWELL   BRO. A. MARSHALL

A most memorable 1978 lodge evening at the Queensway Hall, Dunstable, where we accompanied the reigning English Professional Ballroom Champions, Michael & Vicky Barr, for a cabaret spot.

Robert Wolfe
BLACKPOOL TOWER ORGANIST
INTERNATIONAL RECORDING ARTISTE

Robert Wolfe – talented beyond his years, and as a youngster in Luton, always keen to play in public at every opportunity.

was interpreting other pianists' playing styles, such as Art Tatum, George Shearing, Liberace, Oscar Peterson, Winifred Attwell etc., during a number, and finishing off with his own rendition. He always took a standing ovation for this – his party piece!

Jules of course was used to working the London Hotels where it would be normal for the band to be supplied with interval sandwiches/snacks gratis. Not having them provided on one engagement in a Luton hotel, prompted him to order some, which were duly delivered – as well as the bill! Jules retorted to the waitress "You've got a lot to learn, my dear"! I think as far as Luton was concerned, it was Jules who had a lot to learn!! He again became a great friend over many years.

Weekends were beginning to take on a similar pattern. As there were no 'twists and turns' with personnel, everything had become very stable and consistent and would be until 1974, as will be clarified later. Usually with Friday, Saturday and Sunday engagements every weekend, I would be the first to arrive with drummer Jerry, the music and amplification equipment; Tony would turn up a little later from Stevenage in his Hillman Imp with guitar etc., and with ¼ hr to spare Jimmy and Bob, who had by now become 'travelling companions', would make their entry. We were getting to know each other very well on and off stage, and on stage were able to lean on each other, to get through each evening with the minimum of effort.

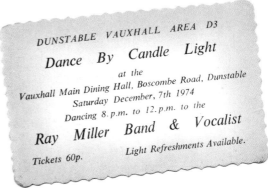

Above and left The large workforce at Vauxhall Motors Luton, and Bedford Trucks Dunstable, generated a tremendous amount of work at the many function halls throughout the area. Here are three, typical of the mid 1970s peak: 1973 at the Hatters Club, Luton; 1974 at the Dunstable Plant Main Dining Hall; 1975 at the Halfway House, Dunstable.

Right 1973 – A village hop for Marks & Sparks; 1970 – The Cement Works, Houghton Regis – long since gone.

Jules Ruben guested with us frequently during the 1970s, as a playing member of the band or cabaret entertainer, on piano and organ. His love was Latin American music and he was in demand by the many Cuban Rhythm Bands, particularly Edmundo Ros at his club 'The Coconut Grove'. He later formed his own 7-piece band called the Latinairs, and broadcast regularly on BBC radio.

In the 1960s Robert and Marguerite O'Hara were British Latin Dance Champions, and personally collaborated with Jules to produce this long playing record.

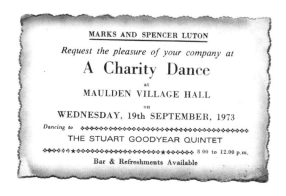

MARKS AND SPENCER LUTON

Request the pleasure of your company at

A Charity Dance

at

MAULDEN VILLAGE HALL

on

WEDNESDAY, 19th SEPTEMBER, 1973

Dancing to

THE STUART GOODYEAR QUINTET

8.00 to 12.00 p.m.

Bar & Refreshments Available

Blue Circle Sports & Social Club

PRESENT

BUFFET & DANCE

at

THE WORKS CANTEEN

on

FRIDAY MAY 29th 1970

Dancing 7-30 until Midnight

to

RAY MILLER BAND

Admission

One weekend is well worth a mention, as we probably set a record for endurance on Fri 1st June, Sat 2nd June and Sun 3rd June 1973. On the Friday we were at the Halfway House for a Dinner/Dance until 1.00am, loaded the hire van, off to Dover for a cross channel ferry, then over to the Hotel Simmer in Ehnen, Luxembourg, where we played for the British Club of Luxembourg who ran a Dinner Dance in honour of Her Majesty Queen Elizabeth II's Birthday on the Saturday. It was at a most beautiful hotel which looked across the River Moselle into Germany. On conclusion it was straight back, wash and brush up, then on Sunday we played for a club night at SKF Leagrave Road Social Club.

Bob Usher on bass guitar was occasionally booked to play with us on the 'bigger' dates, which was the case on this trip to Luxembourg. On the way back we were all starving and, would you believe it, Jerry produced a tin of corned beef and some crackers, to the delight of everyone.

L'Hôtel Simmer vous offre dans un site merveilleux de la Moselle Luxembourgeoise un séjour des plus agréables, aux bords d'une rivière chatoyante, dont les flots scintillent du charme d'EHNEN, réputé par le coloris de ses vignobles et le bouquet de ses vins délicieux, par sa jolie Rotonde et ses ruelles moyenâgeuses, par l'élégance de son sport nautique et la richesse de sa pêche riveraine.

«Wohin?»
«An die Mosel!»
«Also nach **Ehnen!**»

... Und dann stehst du bezaubert in der singenden Rebenlandschaft vor der hellen Häuserfront, der Fluss zieht seine schimmernde Silberschleife, auf der die Wasserskier dahinflitzen, Hügel schwingen moselauf, moselab, uralte Winkelgässchen um die Rundkirche und das Kasino raunen von vergangenen Tagen und stille Höhenwege locken zu besinnlichem Gang. Ein traumschönes Idyll.
Was du suchst, Abspannung, Frohsinn, Freude, du findest es hier. Schlürfe diesen Lebenstrank wie einen Becher köstlichen Weins!
Wer aber Ehnen sagt,

sagt: **Hotel Simmer**

Das Hotel Simmer, die Gaststätte bester Tradition, erlesener Speisen und gepflegter Weine, seit Jahrzehnten weit über die Grenzen hinaus rühmlichst bekannt, bietet auch dir die beglückende Gemütlichkeit des Zuhauseseins. Wenn du je einmal auf dieser schönsten Moselterrasse in geselligem Kreise bei einer Flasche Moseler das Abendwerden im stillen Tal erlebtest, wirst du wiederkehren, immer wiederkehren.

THE **Hotel Simmer** offers a very pleasant stay
in a famous beauty spot of the Luxembourg Moselle, on the banks of an idyllic river whose calm expanse mirrors the charm of the stately, comfortable village. EHNEN, with an old reputation for the subtle fragrance of its vineyards and the characteristic tang of its wines.

for its fine Rotunda in the midst of its old-world alleys and

for the elegance of its aquatic sports and the quality of its river-fishing.

THE **Hotel Simmer** mirrored in the gleaming river in a site of unique splendour and charm.

is proud of the welcome which it can offer to its guests in its lounges and on its terrace;

it is happy to enhance the warmth of its welcome by quality of its food and the distinction of its cellar in an atmosphere of urbane comfort and good-living.

Rutilant des reflets d'un panorama si pittoresque, l'hôtel SIMMER vous réserve, dans ses salons et sur sa terrasse, l'accueil le plus cordial, heureux d'aviver par les fins délices de sa cuisine et de sa cave votre plaisir de vivre.

HOTEL SIMMER

EHNEN-sur-Moselle
(Grand-Duché de Luxembourg)
Téléphone 7 60 30

RESTAURANT 1973
de tout premier ordre
à la carte et au menu

chambre à 1 personne   400.-
chambre à 2 personnes   550.-

chambre à 1 personne av. bain   550.-
chambre à 2 personnes av. bain   850.-
petit déjeuner   inclus

Prix de la Pension: 1/2 p
Chambre, petit déjeuner et deux repas
par personne sans bain   550.- 480
par personne avec bain   750.- 680
en demie Pension réduction de
réductions pour enfant jusqu'à 8 ans ......

Chambres avec balcon, vue sur la vallée
de la Moselle
avec les vignobles en terrasses
Téléphone dans toutes les chambres
La Cave «Aux Millésimes»

Sport nautique

Service et taxes inclus

N: 24

British Club of Luxembourg

[ ] **A Dinner Dance** [ ]

in honour of the Birthday of Her Majesty
Queen Elizabeth II
at the Hotel Simmer / Ehnen
Saturday 2nd June 1973 at 8.30 pm

Dancing to the - Ray Miller Band -

Evening Dress
Optional

Members Ltrs 300
Non-Members Ltrs 350

Our first visit to Luxembourg was in 1973, to play for the British Club, who held a dinner dance in honour of the birthday of Queen Elizabeth II on Saturday 2nd June, at the beautiful Hotel Simmer, Ehnen, overlooking the River Moselle into Germany.

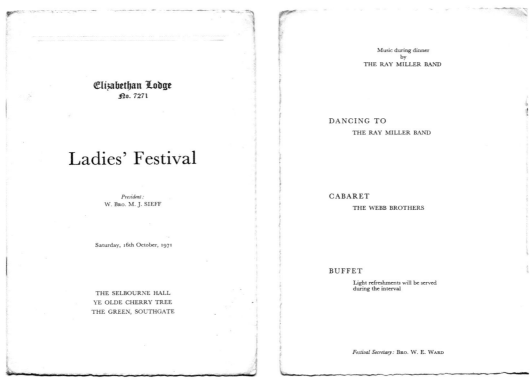

Elizabethan Lodge
No. 7271

Ladies' Festival

President :
W. Bro. M. J. SIEFF

Saturday, 16th October, 1971

THE SELBOURNE HALL
YE OLDE CHERRY TREE
THE GREEN, SOUTHGATE

Music during dinner
by
THE RAY MILLER BAND

DANCING TO
THE RAY MILLER BAND

CABARET
THE WEBB BROTHERS

BUFFET
Light refreshments will be served
during the interval

Festival Secretary : BRO. W. E. WARD

A busy evening in Greater London, playing for dinner, dancing and cabaret accompaniment.

Owing to a similarity in style, we were also jovially called 'the poor man's Joe Loss', because we played a non stop dance programme which to a greater extent consisted of the 'pop' numbers of the day. I took it as a great compliment to be mentioned or thought of as similar to the great Joe Loss Orchestra. We could on the other extreme include many real oldies in some of our medleys because I knew them, and of course I had the sheet music which was largely given to me by Dad from his own pre-war band days.

There was the occasional disaster, none more so than on Sunday 2nd March 1969 when we were booked as a trio at Oxford Dog Track, presumably for lounge music. As Jerry, Tony and myself approached the venue, we saw a hoarding proclaiming the opening of the newly refurbished track and restaurant facilities, and at the entrance, draped across the road, another hoarding also announcing the event, with dancing and music provided by the Ray Miller Showband! We entered the magnificent new supporters' lounge and it was packed, eager no doubt for our arrival. The piano sounded as though it had been outside during the building work — and looked it. It was unplayable, so the only music was rhythm guitar and drums with me singing. Some showband! We got through the evening only with a lot of goodwill all round, and an admission from the management of their mistake with the booking.

The band pictured at the first of our three engagements at the London Hilton Hotel, Park Lane, on Tuesday 30th April 1974. Left to right: Stuart Goodyear (Piano); Jimmy Stead (Tenor Sax); Bob Bates (Trombone); Jerry Blain (Drums); Tony Reynolds (Rhythm Guitar); Bob Usher (Bass Guitar) and special guest on vocals Terri Da Costa.

A growing number of halls had become registered with the Performing Rights Society, which required all bands and performers to list the songs performed, who wrote the words and music, and the publisher. The form was a 2-sided A4 sheet and a real nuisance, but necessary, I guess, to allow royalties to be paid. My completed form would include songs from the 1920s through to the pops of the day.

We started to book female vocalists when it was felt we needed a 'bit of sparkle' on some of the plush engagements we were getting, including three at the London Hilton. It proved a popular move all round, and we continued to use 'only the best' from our professional contacts on a regular basis. We always gave them an enjoyable evening and I know from their response they always looked forward to any future bookings singing with us. The two who slotted in with us perfectly, and were my undoubted favourites because of their overall performance and personality, were Josie Carroll and Pat Barry. At a Licensed Victuallers Ball at the Queensway Hall, Dunstable, Josie gave a performance both during the dinner and afterwards for dancing that was never surpassed.

Second visit to the Hilton, Thursday 7th November 1974.

C&C

CITY OF WESTMINSTER AND BOROUGH OF
CHELSEA LICENSED VICTUALLERS'
HOTEL AND RESTAURANT PROPRIETORS'
PROTECTION ASSOCIATION

Eighty-Ninth Annual Banquet and Ball

President:
G. R. KEWLEY, Esq.
Group Managing Director
Cantrell & Cochrane (Great Britain) Ltd.
Chairman
Cantrell & Cochrane (Southern) Ltd.

THE LONDON HILTON   THURSDAY
PARK LANE, LONDON W1   7th NOVEMBER, 1974

club
SOFT DRINKS

MENU

Oeuf en Suprême Princesse

Truite de Rivière Meunière

Carré de Veau Rôti
Sauce Crème aux Champignons
Boutons de Bruxelles au Beurre
Pommes Parisienne

Orange Givrée

Petits Fours

Café

Music during Dinner
and for Dancing
by the
RAY MILLER BAND

MENU · TOASTS · OFFICERS

YE OLDE FOUNTAINE HOUSE
THE ORIGINAL BRISTOL HOME OF SCHWEPPES

THE LICENSED VICTUALLERS' GOLFING SOCIETY

39th
Annual Banquet & Ball

LONDON HILTON HOTEL
ON TUESDAY 29th APRIL, 1975

Music

During Dinner
and for dancing until 1.30 a.m.

THE RAY MILLER BAND

Third visit to the Hilton, Tuesday 29th April 1975. Dancing until 1.30am – back to Luton 3.30am, off to work 7.30am!!

Above Top freelance London-based vocalist Pat 'Patsie' Barry was a delightful singer, and slotted in perfectly with the band.

Left No picture, but Josie, another beautiful singer, alternated with Pat Barry on those 'special' dance dates.

I often went out on mid-week evenings to visit Social and Working Men's Clubs, to jostle the Entertainment Secs. for Sunday evening bookings, which they gave out well in advance, as they were usually too busy to bother with this at weekends. It was one such trip in 1974 that was to dent the smooth running of the band – as I lost my driving licence.

I had a couple of pints during the evening and, on my way home, stopped at Round Green to get Margaret and myself some fish and chips. Before I reached home everyone was being stopped by the police to check for a stolen vehicle, or at least that's what was said, and the officer smelt alcohol in my car and breathalized me. I was 2 mg over 90! The only consolation was that they accompanied me home with the fish and chips.

Drummer Jerry was unfortunately the immediate casualty, because I could no longer transport him about, in fact, I was finding problems getting about myself. The solution was resolved fortuitously when Kenny Gorrell, another top (ex-pro) local drummer, became available, and he was able to join us immediately on a permanent basis. Ken had a van, and was happy to transport me to the gigs, which was a nice change. Although I was very sad at losing Jerry, life became easier for me, so this cloud did have a silver lining.

Ken was most amiable at all times, and I cannot ever remember him getting ruffled. He was a very colourful character with a dry sense of humour, which made travelling with him most enjoyable (even when I got my licence back), because he always had so many tales to tell about his life as a 'pro musician'. Born in West Hampstead, London in 1929, he was evacuated as a youngster to Bedford in 1939 along with many children, to avoid the bombing, and remembers that some of his schooling was upstairs at the Swan Public House, with a constant smell of beer. He returned home before the end of the war, to witness "Doodle Bugs" and V2 rockets dropping over London.

As a teenager Ken bought his first kit of drums from the PX Canadian Army Stores at Cricklewood, having the desire to become a drummer from his many attendances to see the pit orchestra in action at the Kilburn Empire. His best mate was Harry Hussey, who played accordion and became a life long buddy of Ken's – even up to today, and like Ken moved to Luton, also becoming a household

Kenny Gorrell. A lovely man – and a superb drummer. Joined the Ray Miller Quintet in June 1974.

Above Tickets for the 1980 and 1982 'Bastille Day' Ball at Borehamwood. (Bastille Day is actually 14th July). *Below* Ironic that in 1982 we were also booked for a 'Trafalgar' Ball!

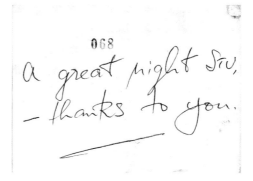

name as a brilliant musician. Ken was initially taught drums by a member of staff from Dr. Barnados who eventually enrolled him into the local Brass Band.

His first break into dance music was as a 14 year old, when the drummer didn't turn up at a "fire station" dance, and his mother suggested Ken, who dropped everything to fill the breach. Because his father had died, Ken was working in a local factory, and pursued his drumming as a semi-pro, but, through going to Archer Street, the musicians' meeting place in London, he received an offer of professional work with top bandleader Harry Leader. Ken played with Harry's band for many years and featured with the band when they did 'live' broadcasts of 'Music While You Work', which was a popular radio programme of the 1940s and 50s, played into factories twice a day, for light relief!

Harry Leader also played at the Holiday Camps around Britain, which was where 'everyone' spent their annual 2 weeks break in the 1950s, and it was at one of these that Ken met his wife Catherine. He also worked with Sidney Lipton and his Orchestra and did a 2 year stint on the liner 'Orcades' with him. Ken took a 9–5 job at NCR, Brent Cross to dedicate more time to his home life, and moved to Luton in 1964, mainly for more affordable housing, and immediately found regular work with the Bill Seaford Trio (keyboards) and Vernon Critten (bass). Ken was always pleased to give percussion tuition to any youngster who genuinely wanted to learn and at 72 still teaches at Luton's 6th Form College and Icknield Arts College, Riddy Lane. He was also someone I rate as a 'special' person and friend, whose unquestioned ability taught me so much.

Complete with boaters, the band at 'the finals' of the Pub Entertainer of the year contest – 1975. L. to r.: Yours Truly (Vocals); Tony Reynolds (Rhythm Guitar); Jimmy Stead (Tenor Sax); Kenny Gorrell (Drums); Bob Bates (Trombone).

PLAYING UP TO A £1,000 PRIZE

A LOCAL group, the Ray Miller Band, swept through to the regional finals of the Pub Entertainer of the Year contest in Luton last night.

The five-piece band was entusiastically received at the Killicks Cottars pub, Sundon Park, and earned maximum marks from three judges and a chance to win the £1,000 first prize at the finals.

The line-up includes vocalist Sutart Goodyear, a mechanical engineer, of Sowerby Avenue, Stopsley; trombonist Bob Bates, engineer, of Wimple Road, Luton; rhythm guitarist Tony Reynolds, an electronics engineer of Collenswood Road, Stevenage; saxaphonist and tenor vocalist and flute player Jim Stead, telecommunication worker, of Montrose Avenue, Luton; and drummer Kenny Gorrell, of Warden Hill, Luton, a professional musician.

Local singer George Arnold, of Roman Road, Luton, also went through to the regional finals.

Left A newspaper cutting from the local evening paper of the time – The Evening Post – July 1975. The pub referred to is now the Purley Tavern, Marsh Farm. (No prizes for spotting the spelling errors!)

It would be wrong to say we had a fan club, but we certainly had a regular number of friends and dancers who followed us to dances at every opportunity. With Jimmy, Bob and myself singing a large percentage of our repertoire, some numbers were becoming regular favourites with our audiences. The two numbers above all that I was associated with were Leapy Lee's 'Little Arrows' (1968) and Tom Jones 'Something 'Bout you Baby I Like' (1974). Whenever we played for a Vauxhall Motors' department do, I always had to sing 'Little Arrows', and when we entered the Pub Entertainer of the Year Competition in 1975, we had to perform non-stop for 6 minutes, so we started with 'Something 'Bout you Baby' as the intro.vocal, which led beautifully into Jimmy and Bob's big blow finale. We kept the same programme and reached the finals in London, which we didn't win, but gave a good account of ourselves, and we did Luton proud in our boaters! The finals were very hectic with the acts following each other on the stage very quickly, and I can never forget hearing for the first time "C'mon now, strike the stage", spoken by the stage manager who wanted us off for the next act!

Another number that I always enjoyed singing over the years, as a twist, was the Vernon Girls 'You know what I mean' (1962), and I usually managed to get Jimmy to play 'It might as well be Spring', as a tenor solo, which was not only one of my favourites anyway, but he played it beautifully and it was the ideal slow foxtrot when the evening needed a 'bit of romance'.

I had 'a bit of Dad' in me, and began to introduce some old favourites into our Barn Dance selection which was a particular favourite at many of our Sunday clubs, such as Welwyn Families; Stotfold W.M.C; T.U.C. Crescent Road, Luton; United Services, Dunstable and above all Russell Park, Bedford. Such numbers as 'Mother Kelly's Doorstep', 'Underneath the Arches', 'Hometown' and 'You made me love you', were sung by the dancers at the top of their voices, and like my mentors 20 years earlier, they changed some of the words to catch the mood such as "You made me love you, you woke me up to do it". The words are actually "You made me love you, I didn't want to do it"! At Russell Park, as soon as I sang the first line, I left them, as one, to sing the second. The Barn Dance seemed to fit into Sunday nights somehow as good fun, where the whole family danced together, and when the dancers went into a progressive Barn Dance, (that is the man moving forward after a sequence) it looked good also.

In November 1976 we were asked to return to Luxembourg to play for the British Embassy who were hosting an International Women's Charity Ball at the European Palace, Luxembourg City, on Saturday 13th. To make the weekend more worthwhile for us, the embassy staff also arranged for us to play at Pub 13, the English Pub, on Friday 12th. The European Palace was a grand marble building, and the guests were the staff and diplomats from all the other European Embassies. Each nationality was asked to prepare food peculiar to that country, for the evening's buffet, and prior to us leaving the U.K. we were asked to take over a quantity of Walls Pork Sausages for the staff to prepare as the British contribution of Bangers and Mash. The various food selections laid out were magnificent, and ranged from dried fish to kebabs. Needless to say the evening was a tremendous success and we were overwhelmed by their collective response.

The reception we received the evening before at the Pub was also tremendous, and we played until 3.00am for dancing, to a truly international audience. One or two singers also came up to sing, and one in particular, an American, was an absolute delight.

A most memorable weekend in November 1976. Friday evening at 'Pub 13', the English pub in Luxembourg City centre, and Saturday at the 'Foyer Europeen' a Grand Palace (as ticket above). The representative buffet of England being bangers and mash.

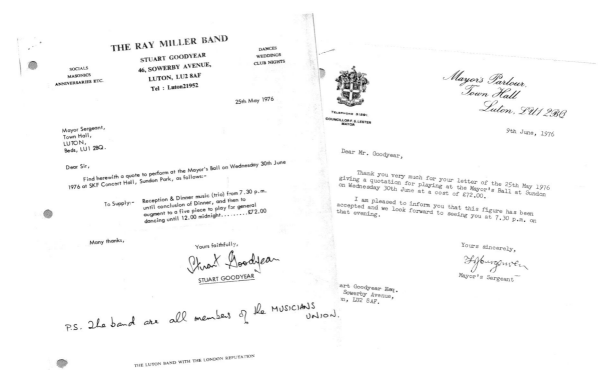

THE RAY MILLER BAND

STUART GOODYEAR
46, SOWERBY AVENUE,
LUTON, LU2 8AF
Tel : Luton21952

SOCIALS
MASONICS
ANNIVERSARIES ETC.

DANCES
WEDDINGS
CLUB NIGHTS

25th May 1976

Mayor Sergeant,
Town Hall,
LUTON,
Beds, LU1 2BQ.

Dear Sir,

Find herewith a quote to perform at the Mayor's Ball on Wednesday 30th June 1976 at SKF Concert Hall, Sundon Park, as follows:-

To Supply:- Reception & Dinner music (trio) from 7.30 p.m. until conclusion of Dinner, and then to augment to a five piece to play for general dancing until 12.00 midnight.........£72.00

Many thanks,

Yours faithfully,

Stuart Goodyear

STUART GOODYEAR

P.S. The band are all members of the MUSICIANS UNION.

THE LUTON BAND WITH THE LONDON REPUTATION

---

*Mayor's Parlour,
Town Hall
Luton, LU1 2BQ*

TELEPHONE 31291.
COUNCILLOR F. S. LESTER
MAYOR

9th June, 1976

Dear Mr. Goodyear,

Thank you very much for your letter of the 25th May 1976 giving a quotation for playing at the Mayor's Ball at Sundon on Wednesday 30th June at a cost of £72.00.

I am pleased to inform you that this figure has been accepted and we look forward to seeing you at 7.30 p.m. on that evening.

Yours sincerely,

[signature]

Mayor's Sergeant

...art Goodyear Esq.
. Sowerty Avenue,
...n, LU2 8AF.

We were receiving some excellent bookings – all needed replies and confirmation, and most of the Luton Civic functions were held at the SKF Concert Hall, Sundon Park or occasionally at the College of Technology, Park Street (now Luton University). The Mayor was Cllr. Frank Lester who dedicated much of his life towards the expansion of Luton Airport, and had the main road through the airport named after him (Frank Lester Way).

All booking and engagement enquiries we were receiving were by personal contact, phone or letter, which needed replies covering quotations or confirmation of same. Over 25 or so years, I must have written thousands of letters. I found out early on that Entertainment Secretaries and Agents were notoriously unreliable, so I would not undertake any booking until I had written confirmation. It held me in good stead many times, when we arrived at a function to find another band there also!

When needed, I did tend to book 'London' vocalists, but there were some excellent vocalists on the local circuit who occasionally sang with us, or were booked to sing as a cabaret spot. Dave Cunningham was a crooner in every sense, with good looks, immaculate black wavy hair, excellent wardrobe, comprehensive library and a superb voice. Singing or not, Dave was always around, whether helping or just showing support, and would sing at the drop of a hat if asked – often for charity. He was a keen motor cyclist and had been a wall of death rider, so it was no surprise when he made a record, relating to his great love, called 'Wall Of Death', which sold well in the local music stores.

It was very gratifying to receive this type of letter! Dunstable was fortunate with the availability of the Civic Centre where most of their functions were held. Can't imagine what the extra payment of £3.00 was for. A round of drinks perhaps.

BOROUGH OF DUNSTABLE

PAMELA M. RADGE, LL.B.

~~L. H. ALLISON, LL.B., L.M.T.P.I.~~

TOWN CLERK AND SOLICITOR

TOWN CLERK'S DEPARTMENT,
MUNICIPAL OFFICES,
76 HIGH STREET NORTH,
DUNSTABLE, LU6 1LF

TELEPHONE: DUNSTABLE (0582) 603166

YOUR REF :

OUR REF :
DWB/VC/1.15.5.2.

When calling please ask for :
Mr. Brooks

18th February, 1974.

Dear Mr. Goodyear,

Civic Celebrations - Staff Supper Dance

I am writing on behalf of the Mayor and the Borough Council to express their sincere thanks to you for the fine performance given by the Orchestra at the Staff Supper Dance last Wednesday evening.

It is felt that it was a most memorable evening and obviously your Orchestra contributed greatly to the success of the occasion. Many members of the Council staff have said how much they enjoyed themselves.

As agreed, I shall be forwarding a cheque in the sum of £3.00 to you in the next few days.

Thanking you once again for all the trouble taken,

Yours sincerely,

P. M. Radge

Town Clerk.

Stuart J. Goodyear Esq.,
The Ray Miller Band,
46 Sowerby Ave.,
Luton.

SOUTH BEDFORDSHIRE DISTRICT COUNCIL

CHAIRMAN OF THE COUNCIL

COUNCILLOR E. S. CLARK

GROVE HOUSE
76 HIGH STREET NORTH
DUNSTABLE
BEDFORDSHIRE
LU6 1LF

Telephone
Dunstable (0582) 603166 (Ext. 202)

10th May, 1977.

Dear Stuart

Silver Jubilee Ball - 6th May

I would like to thank you most sincerely for your services at our Banquet & Ball last Friday evening, which I am sure helped to make it such an outstanding success.

I shall be pleased if you will kindly convey my thanks and appreciation to the members of the Band.

Yours sincerely,

Stuart Clark

Councillor E. S. Clark,
Chairman.

Stuart Goodyear, Esq.,
The Ray Miller Band,
46 Sowerby Avenue,
LUTON, LU2 8AF

1977 – and letters of appreciation were always good to receive.

George Arnold shown here singing on stage at the
SKF Main Hall, Sundon Park.

George Arnold had a beautiful tenor voice and was again always willing, and often sang with us on Sunday evenings at the SKF Social Club, Sundon Park. He progressed through the regional heats to the finals of the Pub Entertainer of the Year competition with us, and as always gave an extremely polished performance, which many thought should have merited him winning. He sang regularly with Geoff Walker at Cesar's Palace night-club and later joined the Harvey Russell Set as their resident singer.

George's two sons David and Les are also very talented musicians, and warrant special mention as 'sons of Luton'. David has become world

famous as a music composer and to date has written music for the films 'Young Americans', 'Stargate', 'Independence Day' and three James Bond movies, 'The World Is Not Enough', 'Tomorrow Never Dies' and 'Die Another Day'. Les is an accomplished drummer and is Musical Director for the Griffin Players, The Luton Light, the St. Andrews Players, the Phoenix Players and the Dunstable Stagecoach!

Frank Philbert was Luton's 'Nat King Cole', who was never without a smile on his face, and again always attended the Musicians Social functions whether to sing or help.

As for the girls, I used Sheila Massey (Luton), Gina Davies (Newton Longville) and Sara Lee (Welwyn Garden City) whose ability, looks and professionalism complemented the presentation of the band on many occasions.

Above Pictured here at the Cresta Ballroom (c. 1960) is another local songstress, Margaret Hall of Runley Road, who established herself as a most competent dance band vocalist, and is pictured here with the Tommy Thompson Orchestra whom she regularly sang with.

Left The Harvey Russell set (early 1980s) l. to r.: Unknown (Bass Guitar); John Hunt (Tenor Sax); John Murray (Alto Sax); John Cook (Trumpet); Mick Coleman (Drums); Brian Sapwell (Trumpet); Peter Ansell (Piano). Soon to join them, as their regular vocalist, was George Arnold.

The Leasiders, at the Biscot Mill 1968, now featured Gillian 'Gill' Evans on vocals. In support: Trevor Evans (Piano); John Goodwin (Trumpet); Bob Bates (Trombone); Dennis Batute (Drums); David Wright (Double Bass). Trevor and Gill were not related.

PRESIDENT'S NIGHT

TOASTS

LUTON NORTH ROTARY CLUB

THE QUEEN   The President

President
Keith White

OUR PRESIDENT   Rotarian Pat Waller
                              Senior Vice President

REPLY   Rotarian Keith White
                                        President

at the
Luton EuroCrest Hotel
Dunstable Road, Luton
16th February 1979

THE LADIES & GUESTS
                    Rotarian Wilson Longden
REPLY   Ann Blight
                  President Luton North Inner Wheel

TOASTMASTER   Rotarian Alan Payne

Dancing to   THE RAY MILLER BAND

The biggest national network of public dance venues was run by Mecca Leisure, and their 'Locarno' at Stevenage (later to become Tiffany's) was the closest to Luton and attracted people from all over the Home Counties. They employed professional bands, and ran a strict dress code for admittance, together with excellent facilities in the halls. We played there on many occasions, where they had a revolving stage for non-stop dancing, which suited our style of playing. I always augmented with Bob Usher (bass) and a female vocalist. I enjoyed visiting the Locarno on my nights off, where I listened to the great Syd Lawrence Orchestra on many occasions.

Right Playing for Mecca Dance Halls was always a prestige booking, and the Stevenage venue was the top local Palais, complete with revolving stage. This Christmas 1975 date had all the trimmings!

MECCACENTRE
Danestrete, Stevenage

Presenting on Weds 17th Dec.

TIFFANY'S
CHRISTMAS
PARTY NIGHT
A SPECIAL DINNER DANCE
WITH ALL THE
TRADITIONAL XMAS FUN
PLUS RAY MILLER
Reception 8.00 pm. Dinner 8.30 pm Prompt.

MENU

Melon O'Porto

Consomme Nice

Roast Norfolk Turkey
with Cranberry Sauce
Chipolata, Bacon Roll,
Stuffed Tomatoes

Chateau & Cream Potatoes
Brussel Sprouts
Vichy Carrots

Christmas Pudding with
Rum Sauce

Coffee & Mints

Balloons
Hats
Crackers
Spot
Prizes
TICKETS NOW ON SALE AT £4.25.

TICKET RESERVATIONS – WEDNESDAY 17th DECEMBER

Name: . . . . Phone . . . .

Address: . . . .

. . . .

Signed: . . . . No. Required . . . . . .

Left 1979 – At the Luton EuroCrest Hotel, Dunstable Road (now the Luton Travelodge). The Rotarians had a busy social calendar.

1981 – For the Hemel Hempstead Lions Club at the Haven Hotel, St Albans.

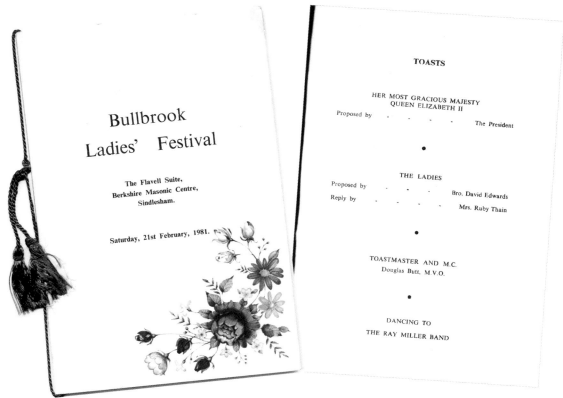

1981 – At the beautiful Masonic Centre, Sindlesham, Berkshire.

As a 5 or 6 piece we could propel our music quite comfortably in most size halls, as the amplification systems were becoming much better, with echo and acoustic facilities helping to enhance the sound. Jimmy used the echo to great advantage when he played his flute, and subsequently received many requests during an evening for 'his' rendition of the popular numbers of the day.

Because of Jimmy's stature, it was always difficult to find a replacement for him

ROTARY CLUB of LUTON NORTH

PRESIDENT'S NIGHT

President
Rotarian Kenneth H. Moores

Chiltern Hotel. Dunstable Road. Luton

Friday. 19th February. 1982

TOASTS

GRACE	The President
THE QUEEN	The President
THE PRESIDENT	Rotarian Geoffrey R. D. Farr Senior Vice-President
RESPONSE	The President
LADIES AND GUESTS	Rotarian Vernon J. Blight
RESPONSE	The District Governor Rotarian K. R. (Bob) Constable (Bushey & Oxhey)
TOASTMASTER	Rotarian Christopher J. Buckingham
Dancing to the	RAY MILLER BAND

1982 – The Rotarians again – this time at the Chiltern (actually in Waller Avenue).

if he was ill or on holiday, so very often I would resort to booking a top London pro if the engagement warranted it, as we did years earlier with the big band. The brilliant Jimmy Skidmore deputised for (our) Jimmy on a number of occasions, and although I would have preferred not to have to book deps., to have the likes of Jimmy Skidmore in the band was akin to playing in a soccer team that included David Beckham or Alan Shearer. He was world famous, having recorded with George Shearing and Kenny Baker and was a member of Harry Parry's Sextet, Eric Delaney's Band, and even more famously Humphrey Lyttelton's. I mustn't forget to mention young Peter Welburn (tenor sax) who also deputised occasionally for Jimmy, and showed true professionalism beyond his years.

CHARTER TRUSTEES OF DUNSTABLE

TOWN MAYOR'S
Charity Dinner & Ball

The Queensway Hall,
Dunstable

Friday, March 16th, 1979
7·0 p.m. for 7·30 p.m.

Reception by:
The Town Mayor and Mayoress
Cllr. and Mrs. P. J. Newton

CABARET

Dancing to the
RAY MILLER BAND

Carriages at 1·0 a.m.

Dunstable Civic functions were keeping us busy!

The friends of the Lady Zia Wernher Centre
for Spastic Children

PRESENT

A GRAND CHARITY BALL

Souvenir Brochure

To be held at

PUTTERIDGEBURY HALL

Friday, February 16th, 1968.

IN AID OF
LADY ZIA WERNHER CENTRE FOR SPASTIC
CHILDREN

THE RAY MILLER BAND

The Ray Miller Band which will be playing for us this evening is well known in the Home Counties for its musical versatility.

The band comprises 5 players and endeavours to only take engagements where all 5 are employed, otherwise it is felt their "sound" may be spoiled.

Their great virtue is their ability to play almost any type of music, whether it be "Olde-Tyme", "Top Twenty" or accompaniment to Cabaret.

The band first started in 1957 made up from employees of Napier/English Electric at Luton Airport. The Manager then, and now, Stuart Goodyear, is the only remaining founder member of the original band.

As semi-professional musicians their achievements these days are comparable with a great many professional outfits and accompany or play with regularly such people as RONNIE CARROLL, GLEN MASON, STAN REYNOLDS, CRAIG DOUGLAS, JOHNNY DUNCAN & MIKE PRESTON etc. With an augmented orchestra they recently played for 'Bob Burgess and Doreen Freeman' at a Ballroom Dancing Exhibition.
The players are:-
TONY REYNOLDS, rhythm guitar. Born in Liverpool, 38 years old.
DEREK HUNT, lead guitar/vocalist. Born in Luton, 33 years old.
JERRY BLAIN, drummer. Born in Luton, 45 years old.
MARK FISCHER, tenor saxophone. Born in Islington, 52 years old.
STUART GOODYEAR, piano. Born in Luton, 28 years old.

THE "VICTORS"

The group was formed in 1963, but has seen several changes in personnel and now has a well formed group consisting of:-
Lead guitarist - Fred Stockley, rhythm guitarist - Pete Wood, bass guitarist - Tony Sear, Drums - Andy Sinclair and Lead singer - Dick Chamberlain. Average age - 21 years.

They have had considerable success, playing as far afield as Towcester, Uxbridge, Baldock, Leighton Buzzard and many local places, entertaining at social clubs, private parties and Hospitals.

These pages and over A selection of dance programmes/tickets from 1968 to 1973. *Above* 1968 – Souvenir brochure – for friends of Lady Zia Wernher centre for spastic children.

Being able to settle into a steady pattern of engagements, with so many of them being repeats, and not having to go out chasing work, made playing so much more enjoyable, and a growing number of our patrons had become personal friends.

Sunday night in particular was a night to look forward to, where we played at Social and Working Men's Clubs and could join the punters in a game of bingo and then afterwards invite volunteer singers from the crowd to "give us a song". The club with undoubtedly the most and best singers on tap was Hatfield British Legion.

I warmed to one or two other characters on the club circuit, one being Sean O'Reilly, a brilliant accordion player at Welwyn Garden City Families Club, who always joined us after the interval to bring in a foot tapping (Irish flavour) finale to the evening.

At Dunstable United Services Club when I vacated the piano to sing at the mic., one of the crowd used to take my seat at the piano and 'pretend' to play. His antics would have you believe he was a virtuoso, even down to playing crossed handed, and soaking up the applause!

Right 1969 – Baldock Round Table.

BALDOCK ROUND TABLE

Adopt

Adapt Improve

No. 781

Ladies' Night

TUDOR SUITE, LOCARNO BALLROOM
STEVENAGE

WEDNESDAY, 19th MARCH, 1969

Chairman: Tabler Derek Oliver

Toast List

THE QUEEN

OUR LADIES
Proposed by Tabler Derek Oliver
Chairman, Baldock Round Table

Reply by Circler Marion Larkinson
Chairman, Baldock Ladies' Circle

TABLE GUESTS
Proposed by William Symonds
President, Baldock Round Table

Reply by Rotarian David Woolven
President, Rotary Club of Baldock

Toastmaster: Tabler John Hall

Dancing until 1 a.m. to
The Ray Miller Band

Below 1970 – Luton Postels Sports and Social Club Dinner Dance.

LUTON POSTELS
SPORTS AND SOCIAL CLUB

TWENTY FIRST ANNUAL

Dinner & Dance

HALFWAY HOUSE HOTEL
LUTON ROAD, DUNSTABLE

Saturday 28th February 1970

6.45 pm for 7.15 pm

Admission by Programme
Thirty Seven Shillings & Sixpence

HER MAJESTY THE QUEEN

Dancing until midnight
to the music of
The Ray Miller Band
With M. C.
Stuart Goodyear

Dance Programme

1 Quick Step
2 Waltz
3 Slow Foxtrot
4 Quick Step (General Excuse Me)
5 Gay Gordans
6 Slow Foxtrot
7 Quick Step
8 Twist
9 Interval Waltz

INTERVAL
and lucky programme number draw

10 Quick Step
11 Old Time
(Valeta and St. Bernard Waltz, Barn Dance)
12 Latin American Cha Cha, Samba
13 Slow Foxtrot
14 Paul Jones
15 Quick Step
16 Slow Foxtrot
17 Party Time
Hokey Cokey, Knees Up, Conga
Charleston, March of the Mods
18 Waltz

THE NATIONAL ANTHEM

THE BAR WILL BE OPEN UNTIL 11.30

THE ROYAL BRITISH LEGION CLUB
— HARPENDEN —

**ANNUAL
DINNER and DANCE**

to be held at "BENNETTS"
on FRIDAY, 26th NOVEMBER, 1971
7.30 p.m. for 8 p.m.

★ Dancing to **THE RAY MILLER BAND** ★

Dancing till 1 a.m.

Tickets £1·50 p each

MID-BEDFORDSHIRE CONSERVATIVE ASSOCIATION
SILSOE BRANCH
present their

Halloween Dance

at
SILSOE VILLAGE HALL
on
FRIDAY, 27th OCTOBER, 1972
9.8 p.m. — 1 a.m.
Dancing to the Ray Miller Band
TICKET 75p includes Buffet

THE ARCADE SADDLERY

DINNER & DANCE

will be held at

THE ANGELS REPLY, HITCHIN,

on THURSDAY, FEBRUARY 1st, 1973,

7·30 p.m. to 1 a.m.

TICKETS - £2·50 each.
Formal Dress.

Above left 1971 – Harpenden British Legion.

Above right 1972 – Mid-Bedfordshire Conservative Association (note price at 75p included buffet) – Silsoe Branch.

Left 1973 – The Arcade Saddlery Dinner Dance at Hitchin.

Below Into the 80s. February at Mitchell Hall, Cranfield.

St. Peter and St. Paul's Lodge No. 1410

Ladies Festival

8th February, 1980

Mitchell Hall, Cranfield Institute of Technology

W. Bro. T. J. Bradshaw, M.B.E., Worshipful Master

TOASTS

The Queen
Proposed by The President

The Ladies
Proposed by Bro. M. J. Cook
Response by Mrs. Connie Bradshaw
Ladies Song, Bro. Bryan Hall

The President
Proposed by W. Bro. K. J. Payne
Response by W. Bro. Tom Bradshaw

Director of Ceremonies, W. Bro. W. T. Wesley

DANCING
to the music of

The Ray Miller Sound

March at the Halfway House.

April at the Halfway House.

DEANSHANGER, WICKEN & DISTRICT
ROYAL BRITISH LEGION

ANNUAL DINNER

Menu & Toast List

KINGSBROOK SCHOOL, DEANSHANGER
7 p.m. for 7.30 p.m.

FRIDAY, MAY 9th, 1980

Again, your Committee extend
greetings to you all and
wish you a happy and
pleasant evening

MUSIC BY
THE RAY MILLER SOUND

LICENSED BAR BY
RUTH & MURRAY
BOOK A BAR
NORTHAMPTON

May at Deanshanger, Northamptonshire.

Tony on rhythm guitar was a brilliant accompanist and had a good ear for 'keys', which made those Sunday soirées so enjoyable for the audience and band alike. I never undervalued Tony's ability on such occasions. I was beginning to enjoy playing music for dinner as much as for dancing, and providing the melody to Tony and Ken's polished backing was always a pleasure. Ken only drank Cokes, but Tony and I discreetly shared many a 7 pint can of beer (Party Sevens) before dancing began.

Opposite above A full evening of music and cabaret, which was so typical of the dinner dance scene in its heyday.

Right and opposite below Lord Carrington was the special guest at this one.

MOULSOE AND DISTRICT FARMING CLUB

21st *Anniversary*

Dinner

January 10th, 1975

MITCHELL HALL
CRANFIELD INSTITUTE OF TECHNOLOGY

THE FARLEY LODGE No. 7796

LADIES' FESTIVAL

President W Bro. Ernest J. Day

HALFWAY HOUSE HOTEL, DUNSTABLE

22nd April, 1977

Entertainment

Music during Dinner and for Dancing
by
RAY MILLER AND HIS BAND

CABARET
'SONGS AND DUETS'
by
DOMINIQUE THIEBAND and JACK CORNWELL
accompanied at the piano by MICHAEL MILLER

TOASTMASTER and M.C.
Ronald Crisp

Festival Committee
W.Bro. R. H. Barrett
  Bro. A. W. Simson

'Happy have we met
Happy have we been
Happy may we part
And happy meet again'

Menu

FRESH WATERCRESS SOUP

★

MIXED SEAFISH BAKED IN ESCALOPE SHELLS

★

PHEASANT A LA MOULSOE
IN RED WINE SAUCE
SEASONAL VEGETABLES

★

GATEAU MILLE FEUILLE

★

CHEESE BOARD

★

COFFEE

★

PORT

Toasts

HER MAJESTY THE QUEEN

Proposed by: B. E. F. HAYNES, ESQ.
(*Club Chairman*)

★★★★★

THE MOULSOE & DISTRICT FARMING CLUB

Proposed by: LORD CARRINGTON, PC, KCMG, MC.
To Reply: B. E. F. HAYNES, ESQ.

★★★★★

THE CLUB'S GUESTS

Proposed by: B. E. F. HAYNES, ESQ.
To Reply: T. GOLLINS, ESQ. (Founder-member)

★★★★★

Toastmaster: T. H. JONES, ESQ.

Dancing till 1 a.m. to
THE RAY MILLER BAND

Dunstable's Civic Centre incorporating the Queensway Hall (c. late 1970s). The superb dance hall housed the most beautiful concert grand piano, but was bulldozed to make way for the Asda Supermarket.

The best piano in the area was undoubtedly the concert grand in the Queensway Hall at the Civic Centre, Dunstable, which was a delight to play. The Civic Centre sadly was closed and pulled down in 2000, and with it went fond memories of so many memorable nights.

It needed to be something special for an engagement to leave a lasting impression, and out of the blue we were booked to play at a re-union Dinner Dance for the 'Girls in Blue' – the Luton Girls Choir at the Ascot Room, Stockingstone Road on 6th September 1974. Before the tables were cleared, at the end of their dinner and completely unrehearsed, one or two of the girls on one of the tables started singing one of their evergreen standards, and within a few bars all the 'old' girls on every table joined in and stood up singing, leaving their partners seated. We were able to accompany them, and there were not too many dry eyes in the room afterwards – mine included.

Opposite 1978 – Carriages at 1.00am from the Queensway Hall, Dunstable, for Dunstable Conservative Club.

DUNSTABLE CONSERVATIVE CLUB

The

Annual

Dinner & Dance

Queensway Hall

Dunstable

Friday 20th January 1978

7.30 p.m. for 8 p.m.

DANCING

to

THE RAY MILLER BAND

Carriages at 1.00 a.m.

Toast List

THE QUEEN

THE CLUB

proposed by
Chairman, South Beds District Council
Councillor S. CLARK

response by
Chairman of Dunstable Conservative Club
A. A. BRIGGINSHAW Esq.

THE GUESTS
proposed by
President of the Club
Councillor C. G. CLARK

response by
DAVID MADEL Esq., M.P.

Menu

Prawn Cocktail
Brown Bread and Butter

Minestrone Soup

Roast Sirloin of Beef
Yorkshire Pudding
Horseradish Sauce
Roast and Boiled Potatoes
Garden Peas
Carrots

Fresh Cream Gateau

Coffee

Looking tired? Perhaps. The band pictured during the interval at the Esso Motor Hotel (now the Chiltern Hotel) Waller Avenue, Luton. Early 1980s. L. to r.: Jimmy Stead; Tony Reynolds; Yours Truly; Betty Estcourt; Bob Bates; Pat Barry; Kenny Gorrell (Betty was vocalist Pat Barry's companion/driver).

The demand from a growing number of our customers was for the latest hit numbers, and, although we were young at heart and always eager to please, more and more of the requests were difficult for us to emulate. Like a good many more entertainers before us, it was time to call it a day while we were still on top, and anyway we were getting tired of the never-ending commitment every week-end. Although the lads continued playing individually in varying degrees, as a band our final engagement was on Christmas Eve 1983 at the Lansdowne Club, Luton.

There are a couple of big bands that I know of locally, who I see advertised to still play in the Glenn Miller and Harry James style, and they are the 'Art Collins Orchestra' and 'Swing's the Thing', so good on 'em!

Opposite 1983 – Typical Friday and Saturday engagements, during our last year together.

ROTARY CLUB of LUTON NORTH

PRESIDENT'S NIGHT

President
Rotarian Geoffrey R. D. Farr

Chiltern Hotel, Dunstable Road, Luton

Friday, 18th February, 1983

TOASTS

GRACE	The President
THE QUEEN	The President
THE PRESIDENT	Rotarian George Ekins Senior Vice-President
RESPONSE	The President
LADIES AND GUESTS	Rotarian John Vincent
RESPONSE	Rotarian David Holborrow
TOASTMASTER	John B. McKean
Dancing to the	RAY MILLER BAND

MANOR OF SWANBURN LODGE

No 8647

LADIES' FESTIVAL

President :

W. Bro. S. J. Wallace

**Saturday
19th February 1983**

**Masonic Hall
Bletchley**

Director of Ceremonies
W. Bro. T. Holderness P.P.J.G.W.

Festival Secretary
Bro. A. Kempster

Catering by
Chefmobile Catering Ltd

Music During Dinner and for Dancing
The Ray Miller Band

Happy to meet
Sorry to part
Happy to meet again

And still going strong. August 11th 2002 at a barbecue in Bob Bates' garden, Harpenden. Top, left to right: George Howden (Trombone); Trevor Evans (Double bass); Brian Jones (Trumpet); Kenny Gorrell (Drums); Andre Beeson (Alto Sax); and hidden behind Andre, Tony Pitt (Guitar). Picture left captures rear view of Bob Bates, who replaced George on trombone, and yours truly sitting, enjoying proceedings.

Somehow I have to find a way to conclude my memoirs, knowing that I have only touched on a fraction of the musicians and characters who kept Luton & District dancing during my lifetime, and knowing also that every musician in every town could tell a similar story. I was not witness to all of the information herein, but have nonetheless relayed it from the many authentic conversations that took place over a pint or cup of tea.

Was it all worthwhile? Well, Toddington couple George and Kath Stewart invited everyone who had been at their wedding in 1970 to their 25th Wedding Anniversary celebrations at Flitton & Greenfield Village Hall in 1995, and included me, as their 1970 band leader, on their invitation list. A gesture which says it all.

Subscription list

Ann Adam
Barbara Adams
Roger Adams
Mrs Rita Arnold
Alena Ayres
Patricia Ayres
Don Barrett
Julie Barrett
Andrea Bates
Bob Bates
Arthur W.Bavister
Mrs Rachel Bell
Barbara B. Bird
Carole and Phil Blain
Connie and Frank Blain
John (Jerry) Blain
Sue and David Blain
Alan and Shirley Booth
Gordon H. Boustred
Margot J. Bramley
Ros (née Goodyear) and
    John Brammer
Dr. A.M.A. Brown and
    Mrs J. Brown
Diane Brown (formerly
    Hutchins)
Mr and Mrs W.S. Brown
    (Bette Lee)
Anne Burley
Vernon Burley
Florence Byrne
Sylvia Chappin
Arthur Claridge
Bryan Clarke
Melvin Colebrook
Tony Coleman
John Collier
Cecilia Eliza Conneely
Michael Christopher
    Conneely
Ruth, Michael, Natasha
    and Bethan Conneely
Margaret and Keith
    Cook
Mary and Hadyn Cook
    (Michigan)
Dave Craddock
Stanley Croft and Joyce
    Ellis

Pamela Currie
D.J. Darby
H.E. Darby
Frank, Anita, Olivia &
    Sophie Di Giacomo
Jill and Robin Dimmock
John Dowson
George Edward Dryden
John W. Durley
Ann and Harry Earl
Ernie Essex
Trevor A. Evans
David Farish
Frank Fay
Mrs D.P. Fischer
Betty Fish
Valerie Fry
Sylvia Gaskell
Mrs E.B.M. Geddes
Mr and Mrs Gilson Lavis
J.R. Glendenning
Diana Ruth Godfrey
Janice Godfrey
Ailsa E. Goodyear
Philippa Claire Goodyear
Kenny Gorrell
John and Jean
    Gouldthorpe
Peter Green
Roger Green
Bob Groom
Mona Rice Grover
Jimmy Harrison
Jack and Audrey
    Harwood
Clifford R. Hawkins
Ivan Hawkins
Joan Hearn
Edna Hendley
David Hobbs
Martin, Kalli and Jo Horn
Catherine Howe
Mrs Peg Hudson
Molly and Harold Hulsey
    (California)
Sheila Humfrey
Harry Hussey
Keith Indge
Barbara and Harry Jarvis
Ron Jeakings
Peter D. Jephson

David Johns
Peter Robert Jones
Valerie and Russ Jones
Brian Keith Joyner (decd)
Roy and Shirley Joyner
Shirley Keech
Maureen and Don Kerins
James Alan Knight
Mrs Pearl Lee
John Leverett
June Loan
Sylvia M. Lovesey
Audrey Ludlow
Luton Sixth Form
    College Learning
    Resources
Mrs Rosalind Mace
Jimmy Marsh
John McLaughlin
Mick Miles
Christopher Morris
John Murray
Musicians Union, Luton
    Branch
Paddy and Bob Norman
Stan and Sylvia O'Flynn
Les Old
Gill and Tony Palmer
Brian James Payne
John and Val Peace
Judith Pedder (née
    Bailey)
Brian and Margaret Perry
Mrs Connie Peters
Bert Poulton
Ronald Edward Poulton
Marjorie Ralley (née
    Cowell)
Peter Randall
Andrew Reynolds
John Reynolds
Paul Reynolds
Thelma Reynolds
Brian W. Rice
Kathleen Roe
Babs Rowe
Joe and Shirley
    Samworth
Brian Sapwell
Janet, Ken and Vicky
    Scott

John Scott
John R. Scott
Bill Seaford
Douglas J. and Roger J.
    Shury
Ray Sills
Mr and Mrs C.P. Sims
Barbara Slaney
Mrs E. Smith (née
    Tufnell)
Harry I. and Mrs E. Smith
Kevin Martin Smith
Leonard G. Smith
Roy Smith
Stuart Smith
Tom Stainsby
Mr J.Stares (decd) and
    Mrs O. Stares
Jim Stead
Lily and Doug Stevens
Bob Stokes
L.J.Strange
Malcolm Sykes
John Tams
Frank Taylor
Tommy Thompson
Kenneth John Tibbs
Maggie Tipping
Paul B. Tipping
Ron F. Walker M.B.E
George Wallace
Margaret (née
    Goodyear) and Les
    Walters
Freddie Wells
Norman Wesley
Wendy and David White
Gerry and Ann Wilkins
Mike Williams
Pauline and Richard
    Willison
Dave Willsmore
Les and Jan Wood
Margaret Woods
Mrs Winifred Wright
Michael, Judith and
    Rebecca Young

WERE YOU BEING SERVED?

Bob Norman

The "nation of shopkeepers" has entered a new era. Our high streets have become impersonal, filled with efficient but bland chain-stores. Gone are the days of the privately-owned stores and shops, when personal service was paramount. Gone but, as far as Luton is concerned, and thanks to this book, not forgotten.

Bob Norman one of their number himself, knew many of those retailers personally. In retirement, he has supplemented his own memories by talking to past employees and family descendants of the original entrepreneurs.

So here are the stories of the traditional chemist, barber, baker, butcher, tobacconist, garage, clothier, jeweller and dozens of other specialists who really knew their trade inside out... and their customers too. A tribute to 50 of Luton's best businesses of yesteryear, profusely illustrated with private and archive photographs, almost all previously unpublished.

STRIKE UP THE BAND
Two centuries of music in Dunstable and District

Anthony J.Ward

In 'Strike Up The Band', the author traces the history of music-making in Dunstable and District from the earliest times where information is available, up to the present day. It is derived from a wider ongoing project by the author.

The book particularly emphasises the history and development of Brass Bands, Orchestras and other groups, recording their contributions to the changing life of the Town and District, and highlighting the various celebrations that have taken place over so many years. The book closes with a series of chapters on the three local Senior Schools in Dunstable with their bands, orchestras and music.

The design of the book is largely based on a collection of photographs and memorabilia, derived from the wide number of contributors having connections with the organisations featured in the book, featuring their recollections of events and personalities. The story of music-making in Dunstable and its surrounding villages is shown in the context of the history of the area and its citizens.

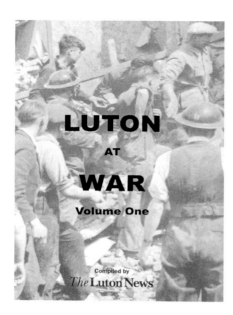

LUTON AT WAR
Volume One & Volume Two

Initially published by the Luton News in 1947, the story of how the people of Luton withstood the dark years of war between 1939 and 1945.

Luton and its population have changed so dramatically in the years since the war that now only a few will recall how the town stood up to the trauma of those war years.

Because of strict war-time censorship much of what occurred during those years was not mentioned in The Luton News. Once the war was over however, The Luton News set about the mammoth task of presenting a complete and vivid picture of war-time life. It tells of the long anxious nights, the joy and the sorrow that made even the most terrifying moments bearable thanks to the tremendous way in which the people joined to help each other.

Written and compiled by the staff of The Luton News at the time, it contains the most comprehensive and fascinating pictorial record. As well as being a moving personal account it is also a unique historical document.

Published in a large format paperback in two parts – volume 1 in autumn 2000 and volume 2 in autumn 2001.

A BRAND NEW BRIGHT TOMORROW…
A Hatter's Promotion Diary

Caroline Dunn

It's a roller-coaster ride being a Luton fan. The one certain thing when you're following the Town is that it'll never be boring.

Follow Caroline Dunn on the Hatters' journey back up to the Second Division, during one of the most exciting seasons in living memory. Villains turned to heroes as the Town completed 2001–2002 with a record breaking run, sealing promotion and netting one hundred goals over the course of the season. Travelogues, match reports and conversations with the players are all included – as well as a certain amount of smugness from the woman who said at the start of the season that Steve Howard, winner of the Divisional Golden Boot, would come good.

From Carlisle to Cheltenham, Darlington to Dagenham, this is a diary of ten marvellous months in the life of a supporter.

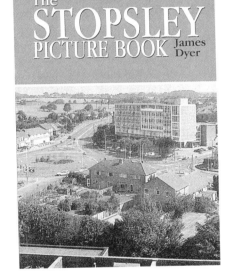

THE STOPSLEY BOOK
THE STOPSLEY PICTURE BOOK

James Dyer

The hamlet of Stopsley, two miles from Luton in Bedfordshire, has a history that stretches back some 300,000 years. Situated in a region initially dependent on agriculture, straw plaiting and brick making, it can be seen as a microcosm of life in almost any village on the northern edge of the Chiltern Hills.

The Stopsley Book tells the story of 20 farms, 16 schools and 4 churches within the civil parish which stretched from Someries Castle in the south to Galley Hill and the Icknield Way in the north. It looks in detail at almost every aspect of village life, particularly in the 19th and 20th centuries, and includes the work of the Parish Council, the weather, water and gas supplies, health care, policing, farm work, brick making and a wide variety of leisure pursuits. Based on thirty years of extensive search and interviews with local people, many now deceased; it is an exhaustive account of a community that still prides itself on its village spirit and individuality.

It includes a collection of 146 photographs, many of which have not been published before.

The Stopsley Book aroused such a great deal of interest in Britain and abroad that a number of readers submitted archive photographs of Stopsley and its surrounding area to the author. These are included in *The Stopsley Picture Book*, which contains 150 photographs and carefully researched captions, to supplement the original work.

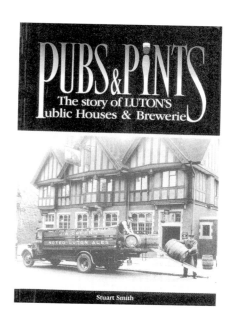

PUBS AND PINTS
The story of Luton's Public Houses and Breweries

Stuart Smith

Whilst the town of Luton is well documented in other ways, this book is the first comprehensive history of its important brewing industry and retail beer outlets – linked, staple trades in the area for over five hundred years.

The development of the modern public house from the early taverns and coaching inns closely followed that of the breweries, with the final decades of the last century seen as the high point in the number of houses licensed to sell beers for consumption on or off the premises. Since then the total has declined with the loss of around 40% during the last one hundred years, most of these losses occurring in the period from 1950 to 1970.

Although documentation dealing with the early breweries and public houses is extremely sparse, it is the intention of this book to try and record the history of each brewery and public house that has had its bearing on the social and drinking pastimes of Lutonians over the last one hundred and fifty years. A special feature of this book is the vast range of three hundred photographs – many old, rare and unusual.

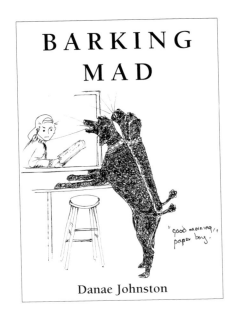

Danae Johnston

"good morning, paper boy."

BARKING MAD

Danae Johnston

Every dog lover between nine and ninety will enjoy following the exploits of Tom and Gill, two delinquent poodles. On their retirement, despite the risk to their prize-winning garden and resident cats, Danae and David rashly take on these canine comedians, their first dogs!

So naïve that they did not know how big the puppies would get, or even that they would need to be clipped at six weekly intervals, the pensioners were to learn everything the hard way – how to deal with scrape after scrape. When Tom jumped the garden fence and returned with one of the neighbours' chickens, for instance! When the dogs herded a flock of sheep into a pond on Christmas Day, or paid an unscheduled visit to a retirement home, or stole the cream from the Jersey milk as it cooled in a bucket on the farmer's kitchen floor, or chased a wallaby at Whipsnade Wild Animal Park – the mischievious adventures go on and on.

Author Danae is a Lutonian, and many of the dogs' exploits are in and around Bedfordshire. Her humorous cartoons and original pithy style make this book a must for all dog lovers. She is also a talented gardener and her garden "Seal Point" has appeared in magazines and on T.V. many times, the most notable being in 1999 when she won the title "B.B.C. Gardener of the Year for the East and South East of England." Many famous gardeners have been to her garden. Geoff Hamilton, back in 1986, Gay Search in 1998, and of course during the recent competition Adam Pasco, Nigel Colborn and Ali Ward as the judges, plus Charlie Dimmock and Alan Titchmarsh, who masterminded the whole show, were around. At certain times her garden is also open to the public to view for charity. And throughout Tom and Gill were never far away!

THE CHANGING FACE OF LUTON

Stephen Bunker, Robin Holgate & Marian Nichols

The Changing Face of Luton traces the fortunes of the settlement and economy of the town from the earliest recorded arrival of people in the area to the present day. It looks at different aspects of Luton and its development rather than giving a straight chronological account of its history.

Luton's roots go back a very long way, yet in less than 200 years it has changed from a small market town to today's busy industrial and commercial centre. This transformation is described, helped by a range of excellent photographs, thereby answering many of the questions frequently asked, and perhaps raising more, about this intriguing town.

The three authors from Luton Museum are all experts in local history, archaeology and industry.

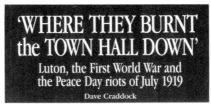

"WHERE THEY BURNT THE TOWN HALL DOWN"
Luton, The First World War and the Peace day Riots of July 1919

Dave Craddock

The weekend of 19/20th July 1919 was arguably the most momentous in the history of Luton. What began as an afternoon of peace celebrations marking the end of the Great War turned into riots that had by the Sunday morning left the Town hall a smouldering, gutted ruin with the military in control of the town. Yet over the years, the story of the riots has been largely neglected.

Drawing broadly on contemporary documents, witness statements and newspaper reports, the book gives a blow-by-blow account of the riots, their aftermath and subsequent trials. The hostility between the Town Council and ex-servicemen's organisations in the preceding months is also covered extensively, as is the impact of the First World War on Luton.

Features of this book include informative appendices containing a wealth of information and over 50 illustrations.

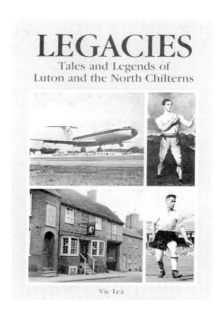

LEGACIES
Tales and Legends of Luton and the North Chilterns

Vic Lea

Vic Lea spent most of his lifetime researching and collecting famous and infamous historical tales of Bedfordshire and Hertfordshire. Following his best selling book, Echoes, here is a further choice of fascinating gleanings from his archives.

Recounted compulsively as only he could, Legacies offers twenty-five gripping sagas of yesteryear... bravery, murder, sport, riot, achievement, disaster, superstition, crime, devilry, transport, danger, intrigue... and many more such dramatic ingredients in an irresistible anthology of legacies from the past.

EXPLORING HISTORY ALL AROUND

Vivienne Evans

A handbook of local history, arranged as a series of routes to cover Bedfordshire and adjoining parts of Hertfordshire and Buckinghamshire. It is organised as two books in one. There are seven thematic sections full of fascinating historical detail and anecdotes for armchair reading. Also it is a perfect source of family days out as the book is organised as circular motoring/cycling explorations, highlighting attractions and landmarks. Also included is a background history to all the major towns in the area, plus dozens of villages, which will enhance your appreciation and understanding of the history that is all around you!